A STUDENT'S GUIDE
TO
ITALIAN FILM

Marga Cottino-Jones
Craig Kelly

University of California
Los Angeles, California

KENDALL/HUNT
PUBLISHING COMPANY
Dubuque, Iowa

B 403041 01

CONTENTS

Preface, **v**

I. Realism and Neo-Realism, **1**

II. Brief Survey of Italian History 1922–1947, **5**

III. Film in Fascist Italy, **11**

IV. Neo-Realism, **17**
    1. The "Great Combat with Truth", **17**
    2. The Major Neo-Realist Directors, **18**
        A. The War: Roberto Rossellini, **18**
        B. The Land: Luchino Visconti, **22**
        C. The City: Vittorio De Sica, **23**
    3. Minor Neo-Realist Directors, **26**

V. The Decline of Neo-Realism, **29**

VI. Revivals of Neo-Realism, **31**

VII. Brief Survey of Italian History 1947–1960, **33**
    1. Post War Italy, **33**
    2. Italian Political Parties, **34**
    3. The Fifties, **36**

VIII. Film in the Fifties, **39**
    1. The Heritage of Neo-Realism, **39**
    2. The Major Directors of the Fifties, **40**
        A. Luchino Visconti, **40**
        B. Roberto Rossellini, **41**
        C. Michelangelo Antonioni, **43**
        D. Federico Fellini, **44**
    3. The "Abandonment of Neo-Realism," **46**

IX. Italian Political History of the '60s and '70s, **47**

X. Film in the '60s and '70s, **49**
    1. Main Trends, **49**
    2. The Major Directors, **50**
        A. Luchino Visconti, **50**
        B. Federico Fellini, **50**
        C. Michelangelo Antonioni, **52**
        D. Pier Paolo Pasolini, **53**
        E. Bernardo Bertolucci, **54**
        F. Lina Wertmüller, **55**
    3. Other Directors, **57**

Notes and References, **59**

Time Line, **61**

Map of Italy, **67**

PREFACE

This hand-book has been written to answer the need 'for an introductory text dealing with Italian film, from Neorealism to the '70s. Books on the subject, although abundant in Italian, are either out of print in the United States or presuppose a cultural and historical preparation in Italian which most college students non-majoring in Italian seldom achieve.

This *Student's Guide* is based on the premise that film is an art form which is very closely related to every day reality. Consequently the appreciation of Italian film is greatly enhanced by a basic knowledge of Italy's political, economic, and cultural history. In this *Guide,* therefore, the students are provided with a brief historical overview of each of the main periods of Italian film with which we are dealing, such as, Neorealism, the Fifties, the Sixties, and the Seventies. Italian film is then discussed in the view of how it relates to the historical background of its time and how individual directors interpret this reality in their own different artistic vision. A Time Line concludes the hand-book, where important historical and cinematic events are listed in chronological order, to help students to grasp visually as well the interrelationship of history and film.

If *A Student's Guide to Italian Film* can assist American students in better understanding Italian culture and appreciating Italian film as one of the many expressions of Italian artistic creativity, we shall have achieved our main objective.

I should like to express our thanks to all of our colleagues and students at UCLA whose encouragement, criticism, and collaboration have helped us to bring this *Student's Guide* to completion. I hope that all the colleagues and students who will be using it from now on will find it useful and worthy of criticism, and that they will share with us their experience and suggestions for improvement.

I would like to express my gratitude to Professor Guido Aristarco from the University of Torino and director of *Cinema Nuovo* for providing the film illustrations; to the *Centro Studi Piero Gobetti* and its director, Ms.

Laura Gobetti, for providing the historical illustrations; and to the Gruppo Editoriale Fabbri, Bompiani, Sonzogno, ETAS SPA, and its Assistant Director, Dr. Giovanni Cobolli Gigli for providing the literary illustrations. My colleague, Professor Pier Maria Pasinetti, has kindly allowed me to use materials relating to his brother, the late Francesco Pasinetti.

Marga Cottino-Jones

I. REALISM AND NEO-REALISM

"Neo-realism," as the term implies, was a new form of realism. Italian neo-realist film is, stylistically speaking, part of a long tradition of realism that includes not only cinema but literature and painting as well. In broad terms "realism" in the arts means an effort to precisely imitate external and historical experience, to make empirical observations and to follow the laws of probability. This description applies as well to the poet Homer as it does to the film director Vittorio De Sica.

In the 18th and 19th centuries, however, "realism" took on a more specific meaning as a result of developments in the novel. In the 18th century English novelists such as Daniel Defoe and Henry Fielding, reflecting the great social and economic changes of their time, began portraying middle and lower class characters in realistic and serious terms, breaking an old convention by which persons beneath the rank of the nobility were considered worthy only of comic roles. This new interest in realism also became an important element of the historical novel created by Sir Walter Scott, who took pains to accurately describe the social milieu embracing paupers and burghers as well as kings. Scott was to influence Italy's Alessandro Manzoni (1785–1873) whose classic novel *I Promessi Sposi (The Bethrothed)* contains a wealth of serious characters of all classes.

France in the 19th century produced two great novelists in the realist style: Stendhal and Balzac. Stendhal is the key figure. In his classic novel *Le Rouge et Le Noir (The Red and the Black,* 1830) the effort to portray characters of all classes immersed in a convincing, realistic background reaches an unprecedented intensity. Today we take such realism for granted, and it is easy to assume that literature has always been this way. But as Erich Auerbach, in his classic study of realism in Western literature *Mimesis,* has said, "Insofar as the serious realism of modern times cannot represent man otherwise than as embedded in a total reality, political, social and economic, which is concrete and constantly evolving—as is the case today in any novel or film—Stendhal is its founder."[1] Henceforth most novelists tried to give the impression of representing the hazards of everyday life in an objective style unmarred by the author's interpretation. Stendhal himself said, "Je prends au hasard ce qui se trouve sur ma route." ("I take at random that which is found along my path.")

An extreme form of realism called "naturalism" also developed in the 19th century. Its founder was the French writer Emile Zola. Naturalism not only tried to observe reality accurately, it also boasted a scientific objectivity on the part of the authors and stressed the causal relation between the environment and a character's actions. In Italy the Sicilian Giovanni Verga (1840–1922) influenced by both the French realists and naturalists developed the style called *Verismo. Verismo* was similar to naturalism but did not accept naturalism's "scientific" language. Together with the specifics of environment, Verga also emphasized the strong primitive impulses and passions of his Sicilian peasants. Verga is considered one of the greatest novelists of the 19th century and his influence on twentieth century Italian literature and film has been profound.

The United States entered the realist scene in the twentieth century with such writers as Sherwood Anderson, John Dos Passos, William Faulkner, Ernest Hemingway and John Steinbeck.

1

Portrait of Giovanni Verga (1840–1922) at age 73.

Their influence in Italy was great, and two of Italy's best known writers, Cesare Pavese and Elio Vittorini led the translation and promotion of American classics. The American model in Italy was important for a number of reasons. Politically, many Italian authors in the 1930's saw their admiration for American literature as a quiet protest against the fascist dictatorship of Mussolini (in power from 1922 to 1943). Furthermore, the Italians admired the spare, non-rhetorical style of the American authors and the way they dealt frankly with any subject matter, regardless of how common, grim or violent.

This American realism and its English, French and Italian antecedents, contributed to the rise of a group of Italian novelists and short story writers called "neo-realists": interestingly enough the term neo-realism was applied to literature retroactively, only after it had been used for Italian film of the late 1940's and early 1950's. The neo-realist school of literature is not as well defined as its counterpart in film but among its writers we can include the above mentioned Cesare Pavese and Elio Vittorini, as well as Vasco Pratolini, Ignazio Silone and Carlo Levi. Neo-realist prose was characterized by a low-key opposition to Fascism, a concern for the problems of industrial workers and peasants and the use of lower class as opposed to aristocratic heroes. With respect to style neo-realist prose rejected rhetorical affectation and described the settings and events of day-to-day life in frank terms, often reproducing the popular speech of the protagonists. All of the neo-realist writers seemed to carry out Stendhal's dictum of "taking whatever is found along the way." In fact two of Pratolini's novels contain the word *Cronaca* (literally "chronicle") in the title. Several of the neo-realist literary works achieved international fame. Vittorini's *Conversa-*

zione in Sicilia (*In Sicily*, 1941) and Pratolini's *Cronache di poveri amanti* (*A Tale of Poor Lovers*, 1946) were widely translated. Silone wrote two anti-fascist novels that had great success in the United States: *Fontamara* (1933) and *Pane e vino* (*Bread and Wine*, 1937). Levi, a Jewish doctor and painter, was sent by Mussolini into "internal exile" in the tiny village of Aliano in Southern Italy. He wrote about his experiences among the poor people of Aliano in the very popular *Cristo si è fermato a Eboli* (*Christ Stopped at Eboli*, 1946). *Fontamara, Bread and Wine* and *Christ Stopped at Eboli* all describe in frank and sympathetic terms the poverty and ignorance that afflict Southern Italy. In so doing they criticize the Fascist government for its exploitation of these people. Their criticism, however, is mostly in terms of an objective description of the dismal conditions of the Southern workers, marked by profound compassion for their suffering and humiliation. Nowhere do we find blatant anti-fascist propaganda or self-indulging moralistic rhetoric. These novels succeed in "letting the facts speak for themselves." The neo-realist writers, like Stendhal, wrote works that were steeped in politics. And like Stendhal, the neo-realists knew how to separate politics from propaganda.

With such a rich realistic tradition preceding it one may justly ask what is "new" about Italian neo-realist cinema. Not only did the Italian neo-realist phenomenon in film occur after nearly two centuries of realism in the novel and short story, but many examples of realism in cinema had appeared before Italy's celebrated cinema movement. To discover what is new about Italian neo-realism (and from here on the term will apply to film, not literature, unless otherwise indicated) we must turn briefly to Italian history of the period 1922 to 1947, that is, Italy during the Fascist regime of Mussolini, during World War II and the Liberation, and during the immediate post-war period. Few movements in the history of literature or film have been so closely tied to their contemporary political situations as Italian neo-realism. As the famous French film critic André Bazin said, "Some components of the new Italian school existed before the Liberation: personnel, techniques, aesthetic trends. But it was their historical, social and economic combination that suddenly created a synthesis in which new elements also made themselves manifest."[2]

II. BRIEF SURVEY OF ITALIAN HISTORY 1922–1947

In 1870 the Italian peninsula became united as a constitutional monarchy with a king, prime minister, and a two-house legislature of Parliament. Italian society of the late 19th and early centuries presented an uneasy mixture of a patriarchal rural society and a rapidly expanding urban industrial network. Other countries, such as Great Britain, that had been faced with this conflict had managed, despite enormous economic hardship suffered by the industrial poor, to avoid major political upheaval because they had a long tradition of parliamentary government and a large middle class that supported parliamentary democracy. Italy's parliamentary tradition was, on the other hand, very young, and its middle class was still relatively small, so the division between urban and rural societies was more pronounced. This bifurcation was compounded after World War I (1914–1918) by the large number of veterans returning from the front who either could not find jobs or were no longer satisfied with their former peace-time occupations. Furthermore, many Italians were angry because the Paris Peace Conference following the war failed to grant Italy the territorial concessions it had been promised in the Treaty of London of 1915. This prompted the phrase, "We won the war but lost the peace." For these and other more complex economic reasons, Italy was in great turmoil between 1919 and 1922. The first political force to take advantage of the instability was the Socialist Party, which increased its membership and supported strikes in Turin and Milan, Italy's two industrial centers. But a series of rifts in the Socialist leadership (the most pronounced led to the formation of a new party, the Italian Communist Party, in 1921) rendered the left incapable of profiting from the political and economic tension. On the other hand the government, led by the Liberal Party, failed to secure a peaceful solution and Italy seemed ripe for take over by a "strong man" who could promise the formula of "law and order." This man was to be Benito Mussolini, a former Socialist who had broken with the party in 1915 and had formed the *fasci di combattimento,* groups of armed political units that eventually formed the Fascist Party. From 1919 to 1922 the Fascists openly opposed the Socialists and Communists, often violently. Support for the Fascists grew and in October of 1922, following a bloodless *coup* called the "March on Rome," Mussolini was asked by the king to replace Luigi Facta as prime minister. The Parliament voted Mussolini full powers, obviously unaware that it had just invited in a dictatorship that would last 21 years. Mussolini's appeal was based mainly on his promise of a "return to order," an end to strikes, an end to the "fear of Bolshevism," a reassurance to the new middle class that they would not become "proletariarized," and finally, a promise that Italy through a dedication to military virtues could become a Great Power and re-evoke the Roman Empire (the term Fascism comes from the Latin *fascis,* a symbol of authority of the Roman Emperors). In his first few years in power Mussolini (often called "Il Duce", "The Leader") moved cautiously, clearly trying to reassure Italians and the rest of the world that his intentions were not dictatorial. But after surviving a crisis in 1924–25 involving the murder of the Socialist Parliament member Giacomo Matteotti who had opposed the Fascists, Mussolini unhesitatingly asserted his power, reducing the government to a single party and developing a system called corporatism. Corporatism, which developed gradually and finally crystalized into the "Chamber of Fasces and

Corporations" in 1938, professed to be a system in which political representation was based not on one's residence, but on one's occupation, e.g. agriculture, transport, manufacturing, etc. Supposedly such a system would have eliminated class conflict. In practice corporatism allowed the Fascist Party to maintain rigid control over the unions (eliminating the old Catholic and Socialist union groups), while greatly favoring big business. As historian H. Stuart Hughes concludes, "From the overblown verbiage of corporatism, then, only two realities emerge: the political dictatorship and the strong position of the employers. The rest was wind. The elaborate corporative machinery served largely as a facade to lead the outside world—and even, perhaps, some people in Italy— to believe that Mussolini had eliminated class antagonism in his new state. In actuality, below the surface of apparent harmony, the conflict of class interests raged as bitterly as before."[3] Mussolini had presented his regime as a revolutionary one, but as Hughes goes on to say, it was simply a "conservative regime in revolutionary clothing." This is not to deny the fact that Mussolini achieved some successes such as controlling inflation, draining marshes and improving transportation. But these things alone were hardly revolutionary. The worst of Italy's problems were ignored or exacerbated by Mussolini's patchwork.

By far Mussolini's worst offense was leading Italy into the Second World War on the side of Nazi Germany. In fairness it must be said that Mussolini's motives were not primarily an ideological identification with Adolph Hitler, but rather the fact that Mussolini saw in the "Rome-Berlin Axis" a chance for Italy to achieve Great Power status. This desire had only partially been satisfied by Mussolini's invasion of Ethiopia in 1936 and the claim that the "Roman Empire" had

Tecnosound

Benito Mussolini, the leader of Fascism.

6

been re-established. Italy's ties to Germany strengthened in the late 1930's as both countries assisted Franco's nationalist forces in the Spanish Civil War. As World War II broke out, Mussolini at first kept Italy out of the conflict, but Hitler's early string of successes (Poland, Denmark, Norway, Belgium, France) convinced Mussolini that if Italy were to gain anything from the war, immediate entry was imperative. Mussolini overrode the advice of his top generals that Italy was not yet adequately prepared militarily. The generals were right and the war went badly for Italy. When in July of 1943 British and American (the "Allied") forces overtook Sicily, many in Italy's high command were convinced that Mussolini had to go. On July 25, 1943 King Victor Emmanuel III asked for Mussolini's resignation. Mussolini was arrested and imprisoned only to be rescued shortly afterward by the Nazis. The chaotic period between July 25, 1943 and September 8, 1943 is known as "the forty-five days." During this time, Marshall Badoglio, who had replaced Mussolini, walked a tightrope by trying on the one hand to secretly negotiate an armistice with the British and American forces while at the same time trying to convince Hitler that Italy was still on his side. An armistice was finally signed: Italy had switched sides. Unfortunately the armistice

Centro Gobetti

The news of Mussolini's execution on the paper L'Opinione of April 30, 1945.

7

was not well planned and when it was announced on September 8th, neither the Anglo-American forces, nor the Italians were able to prevent the Germans from occupying Italy all the way down to Naples (see map). This initiated two of the most tragic years in modern Italian history. From 1943 until 1945 when World War II ended, Italy was divided in half. In the north ruled the Germans and those Italians who remained loyal to Fascism. Mussolini had been re-established as a figurehead leader of the zone called the "Italian Social Republic" or the "Republic of Salò" (from the place where Mussolini had his headquarters. The ambiguity of the term Italian Social Republic is matched by the neo-fascist movement in Italy today which is called the "Italian Social Movement"). The South was under Allied control with the co-operation of Marshall Badoglio and the king, both of whom had fled Rome after September 8th. Italian history from late 1943 to April 1945 is largely a story of the Allied forces' gradual push toward the North until the Nazis were finally ousted completely. An important part of the Allied success was due to the Italian underground resistance movement that arose during this time in the Nazi-controlled zone. The efforts of these so called "Committees of National Liberation" (CLN) had three very important results. First of all they greatly weakened Nazi control in the North and helped prepare the way for the Allied troops to push northward. Secondly, their almost legendary efforts helped regain international respect for Italy, respect which had been lost by the alliance with Hitler. Thirdly, the success of the underground resistance added significantly to the prestige of the Italian Communist Party which had provided much of the resistance leadership (a parallel situation existed in occupied France). By April 1945 the war was over. Mussolini tried to escape incognito into Switzerland but was recognized and taken to Milan and executed.

In the immediate post-war period, two major political facts concern us: first of all, Italy was in a state of destruction and chaos as a result of nearly two years of bloody warfare on its own territory. The economy was in a shambles, industrial centers and transportation routes had been heavily bombed and unemployment was high. But, (and this is the second major political phenomenon) along with this grim situation went a strong current of hope that out of the ashes would arise an Italy that would be economically strong and socially just, (creating a more equal distribution of wealth). The successes of the left during Italy's struggle for liberation helped encourage this hope, as did the proven co-operation between Catholics and Communists during the Resistance.

This latter fact brings up an important point. The Italian Communist Party had, as one of its founders, a thinker who is often regarded as the most important Marxist ideologue since Lenin. His name was Antonio Gramsci. Gramsci was born on the impoverished island of Sardinia in 1891 and studied in Turin where he became a noted Socialist journalist. The Italian Communist Party was formed in 1921 and Gramsci was soon to become its first Secretary General. He was imprisoned by Mussolini for ten years and died just after his release in 1937 thus becoming a martyr to the cause of Italian Communism and a great inspiration to the Resistance. While in prison Gramsci had written extensively on a myriad of subjects, particularly Italian cultural and intellectual history and the possibilities of a Marxist revolution in Italy. These writings have been collected in the so called *Quaderni del carcere (Prison Notebooks)*. He tried to develop an "Italian Marxism" which would apply to Italy's unique social and economic situation. This required dealing with two topics which are not found in Marx. First of all Gramsci saw the need for developing a revolutionary strategy that would involve not only the industrial proletariat (the vanguard of Marx's revolution) but the peasantry as well. Gramsci knew that in Italy no revolution could succeed without taking into account the enormous rural work-force.

Italy also presented a second unique phenomenon: regionalism. Before its political unification in 1870 Italy was a conglomeration of independent states, many of which were under foreign domination. This division could not simply be swept away by a political act (the unification of 1870) and therefore Italy has continued even to this day to present significant regional differences. Gramsci saw that Marxism in Italy would have to deal with the complex cultural problems of regional differentiations.

All in all Gramsci envisioned the revolution in Italy not as an explosive *coup d'état* but as a very gradual cultural re-orientation. Gramsci's long-term strategy became the official stance of the Italian Communist Party so that, under Gramsci's successor Palmiro Togliatti, the Party (known as the PCI in Italy) was ready to engage in democratic compromises with other Italian political parties such as the Christian Democrats, the Socialists, the Republicans, the Liberals and so on. This attitude contributed greatly to the post-war reformist optimism in Italy.

Optimism and solidarity seemed to find concrete expression in the coalition government formed in December of 1945. This government combined the Christian Democrats (the largest party, which thus supplied the Prime Minister Alcide De Gasperi), the Communists, the Socialists and the moderate Republicans. In 1946 Italy in a referendum officially became a Republic, casting off the old monarchy. It appeared that a political mechanism existed to make long-needed social reforms and an atmosphere of hope prevailed in Italy through the first half of the year 1947. What occurred after that will be discussed in Chapter VII.

10-11   Committees of National Liberation

2-3   Committees of National Liberation

                          Italian Social Republic

Committees of National Liberation

III. FILM IN FASCIST ITALY

"Cinema is the strongest weapon"
Benito Mussolini

Literary tradition and the specific socio-political situation of Italy between 1919 and 1945 seem to be the most influential factors for the development of Italian neo-realist film. And yet a discussion of the origins of neo-realism would not be complete without an examination of the film industry in which the neo-realist directors first gained their experience. This, of course, was the film industry of the Fascist regime.

As the quote at the top of the page indicates, Mussolini was greatly impressed with the political potential of film and he did everything possible to exploit that potential, especially in the later years of the regime. In 1937, 32 films were produced in Italy. In 1942, that figure ran to 119. One might imagine that Mussolini, in his desire to profit from the advances in film technology, exercised rigid control and censorship over the industry. This is true to an extent, but at no time did the regime's demands equal those of the Nazi government on the German film industry. On the whole, Mussolini encouraged Italian directors to make films that showed Italian life in a positive light, and after Italy's military expeditions in Africa began, Mussolini ordered propaganda-style films celebrating the Italian armed forces. Yet intellectuals like Luigi Chiarini, Umberto Barbaro and Francesco Pasinetti were able to continue their discussions of film theory relatively freely. Film directors who did not wish to blatantly praise the regime could make films that were politically "neutral." This could be done in a number of ways. One way was comedy, long a rich tradition in Italian theatre and now ready to be transferred to the screen. The leading comic director in Fascist years was Mario Camerini who is also known for having launched Vittorio De Sica as an actor. Camerini's popular films include *Uomini che mascalzoni!*, (*Men, What Scoundrels!*, 1932), *Darò un milione*, (*I'll Give a Million*, 1935) and *Il Signor Max* (1937).

Another avenue by which directors could avoid explicitly supporting Fascism was the historical or pseudo-historical spectacular film. This genre also had a long tradition in Italy, for this was one of the types which dominated the silent films of the pre-World War I era. The master of the historical spectacular in the Fascist era was Alessandro Blasetti, whose *La Corona di Ferro* (*The Iron Crown*, 1940) was enormously popular and won the Grand Prize at the Venice Biennale in 1941.

Mussolini's encouragement of the Italian film industry took concrete form in the film institutes, schools and journals that he established during his regime. In 1925 he set up L.U.C.E. (L'Unione Cinematografica Educativa) an educational film organization which eventually made propaganda documentaries such as *Il Duce*. More importantly Mussolini established the film school C.S.C. (Centro Sperimentale di Cinematografia) in 1935. The first president of C.S.C. was the noted film theorist Luigi Chiarini. Joining him in lecturing at the school were Umberto Barbaro, Alessandro Blasetti and Francesco Pasinetti. Pasinetti had contributed greatly to film study in Italy by being the first person to write a doctoral thesis on film. In 1938 he completed the first

Italian Silent Film: *Cabiria* (1914).

Italian Silent Film: *Assunta Spina* (1914).

history of cinema ever written in Italian, *Storia del cinema dalle origini ad oggi (A History of Cinema from its Origins to the Present)*. The C.S.C. numbered many important future directors among its students, including Giuseppe De Santis, Luigi Zampa, Pietro Germi, Roberto Rossellini and Michelangelo Antonioni. In 1937 the C.S.C. began publishing a film journal *Bianco e Nero*.

Besides *Bianco e Nero* another important film journal was established under the aegis of the Fascist regime: *Cinema* in 1935. The director of the journal was Mussolini's son Vittorio. Despite the visible connection to the Fascist regime, *Cinema* was soon dominated by writers with leftist political views, including the above mentioned De Santis and Antonioni as well as the great director-to-be Luchino Visconti.

One of the most important aspects of the journals *Bianco e Nero* and *Cinema* was that they both called for a more realistic style of film. While such articles were theoretical enough to avoid censorship, they did have a great influence on the later neo-realist directors. Among the writers of *Cinema* the influence of Italy's great realist writer Giovanni Verga was so great that *Cinema* was often called "the Verga group." One article in *Cinema* praised Verga's "virgin, bare, violent language" (November 25, 1941) while another called Verga's work "revolutionary art inspired by humanity that suffers and hopes," (October 10, 1941). The latter description will aptly apply as well to neo-realist films. In short, the *Cinema* group wanted to rejuvenate Italian cinema by modelling it after Verga's prose. As critic-director Antonio Pietrangeli said, "There is no renewal

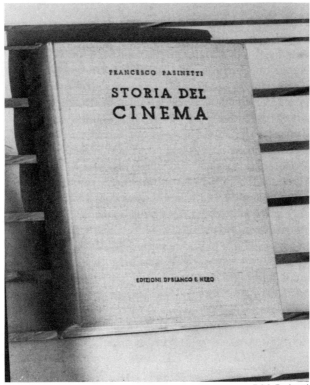

P.M. Pasinetti

F. Pasinetti's *History of Cinema*

without realism." Yet, even though the *Cinema* ideal was far removed from the majority of Italian films being made at that time, one can find a realistic trend in certain sectors.

One example is the documentary film including the works of Rossellini *La nave bianca* (*The Hospital Ship,* 1941), Antonioni *Gente del Po* (*The People of the Po Valley,* 1943) and Pasinetti *Venezia Minore* (1942 and other documentaries on Venice). In fact Pasinetti's refusal to accept the sharp distinction between documentary and fictional film narratives (as he demonstrates in *Il canale degli angeli, The Angels' Canal,* 1934) prepares already for what will be the quasi-documentary style of most neo-realist films.

Furthermore, the search for models of cinematic realism led many Italian directors and critics to look abroad, to Russia and particularly to France. Three French directors had great influence on the Italians: René Clair *À nous la liberté* (*Freedom For Us,* 1931); Marcel Carné *Quai des brumes* (*Port of Shadows,* 1938), *Le jour se leve* (*Daybreak,* 1939); and Jean Renoir *La Grande illusion* (*The Grand Illusion,* 1936), *Regle du jeu* (*Rules of the Game,* 1937).

Italian admiration for French realist cinema was to cause tension with the Fascist regime, however. Realism was out of step with the Fascist idea of what cinema should be, and the French themselves were to become enemies of the Rome-Berlin Axis. This tension reached a dramatic climax at the Milan Triennale of 1940, just before the Nazi invasion of France. At the Triennale Alberto Lattuada, Luigi Comencini and Mario Ferrari arranged a showing of Jean Renoir's anti-war classic *La Grande illusion.* The film was enthusiastically received but the Fascists were upset

Cinema Nuovo

Luchino Visconti's *Ossessione* (1942).

by the pro-French, anti-war attitude of the spectators and fighting broke out. The police arrived and Lattuada narrowly escaped arrest.

Despite occasional incidents of this sort, the discussion about realism continued in Italy. Eventually there were some encouraging results, even in the midst of World War II. In 1942, Alessandro Blasetti made the famous *Quattro Passi fra le Nuvole (Four Steps in the Clouds)*, which although a comedy, dealt frankly with the problems of working people. In the same year, Vittorio De Sica directed *I Bambini ci Guardano (The Children are Watching Us)* which portrayed the breakup of a family seen through the eyes of a child and rejected the Fascist regime's attempt to portray the bourgeoisie in ideal terms. Visconti's *Ossessione (Obsession, 1942)* based on James Cain's novel *The Postman Always Rings Twice*, presents a very realistic view of the lower classes in the Po Valley region of Northern Italy and pays close attention to environmental detail. The film, which involves a love triangle and a murder, was so unflattering in its treatment of daily life in Italy that Mussolini, although first approving of it later ordered it destroyed. Fortunately Visconti himself had kept a copy.

The movement toward realism that was evident in *Four Steps through the Clouds, The Children Are Watching Us* and *Ossessione*, often called "precursors of neo-realism", was cut short by the chaotic events of 1943–1945 which put a halt to film production. The end of the war in 1945 meant the beginning of the next step in the realist movement: neo-realism itself.

IV. NEO-REALISM

1. THE "GREAT COMBAT WITH TRUTH"

The neo-realist film movement rushed into Italy on the heels of the departing Nazi troops. The sense of relief coming from the realization that Mussolini, the Fascists and the Nazis had been defeated was matched only by a conviction that the story of widespread suffering needed to be filmed immediately. Hence Rossellini's *Rome Open City,* generally considered the first neo-realist film, was made in 1945, the same year the war ended. In the next six years, the neo-realist movement was to produce several of the finest films in the history of world cinema.

Each individual neo-realist director had his own particular interests. Rossellini was most concerned with the upheavals of the war itself. Visconti addressed the problems of the peasantry. Poverty in the inner city became the favorite theme of De Sica. Yet despite these varied emphases, certain generalizations do apply to the neo-realist movement as a whole.

More than any one stylistic element, there is a certain attitude which best describes neo-realism. That attitude includes a strong desire to uncover the truth about the widespread suffering in Italy, and to identify sympathetically with the plight of the victims. Neo-realism is an attack on individualism in the negative sense, that is the view of society as a mere collection of individuals. Individualism of this sort defines morality in negative terms, "I can do whatever I wish as long as I do not hurt anyone." But such a view condones indifference to others, a satisfied ignorance of others' suffering. It is that indifference and ignorance that neo-realism addresses. Cesare Zavattini said many of our problems exist because we simply are not aware of the plight of others. Neo-realism wants to help overcome this barrier by showing us how others live, suffer and hope.

Naturally the neo-realist project would have to involve filming situations which were not always pleasant or "beautiful". The journal *Cinema* in October 1943 carried this statement by Italy's famous literary scholar Francesco De Sanctis, "It is said that the ugly is not material for art and that art represents the beautiful. But . . . there is nothing that is in nature that cannot be in art." De Sanctis (not to be confused with the director Giuseppe De Santis) was very influential among the *Cinema* group and his above quoted statement helped provide aesthetic justification for neo-realism's desire to portray poverty. De Sanctis' words were echoed later on by the director Alberto Lattuada in what may be called the "neo-realist manifesto,": "So we're in rags? Then let us show our rags to the world. So we're defeated? Then let us contemplate our disasters. So we owe them to the Mafia? To hypocrisy? To conformism? To irresponsibility? To faulty education? Then let us pay all our debts with a fierce love of honesty, and the world will be moved to participate in this great combat with truth."[4]

When Cesare Zavattini was accused of being exclusively concerned with portraying a poverty and misery-stricken Italy he replied, "We have started with misery simply because it is one of the most dominant aspects of our present society."[5]

Rossellini, when asked to define neo-realism, called it "an interior state, a way of feeling, a humble representation of the world, an act of courage that aspires to accept man as he is."[6]

What is common about all of the above descriptions of neo-realism is the clear sense they convey of a "mission". Neo-realist directors and theorists saw the movement as a social as well as aesthetic force. Another statement by Zavattini is revealing: "To describe poverty is to protest against it." Neo-realism was a cinema of protest, of liberation not only from Fascism but from injustice in general. Neo-realist directors hoped that by warmly identifying with victims of suffering that they could instill in their viewers a positive response, a movement toward reform. That they were able to seek such a response without turning their films into propagandistic documentaries is to the credit of neo-realism.

This, then, is a major element of the "newness" of the "new realism," the strong commitment to the immediate socio-political situation. Never before had a realist movement in film or literature been so attached to the contemporary political situation as to actually encourage a reform of that situation. But the greatness of neo-realism lies in the fact that it managed to extract from the accurate and detailed portrayal of the contemporary Italian socio-political situation universal and timeless themes. The classic neo-realist films have as much to tell us today as they did then. De Sica's *Bicycle Thieves,* besides addressing the problem of unemployment in post-war Italy, invites us to identify with all victims of social and economic injustice. In summation, what most characterizes the movement is, as Bazin says, its "fundamental humanism." As different as the various neo-realist films are, they all share the mission of inviting out solidarity for those who "suffer and hope."

Given this common mission it is not surprising that there are many stylistic similarities among the neo-realist films. Briefly these include the almost exclusive use of on-location shooting in authentic settings, the use of non-professional actors, an emphasis on popular speech, a rejection of elaborate or contrived plots, frequent employment of improvisation. Certainly some of the neo-realistic techniques were developed out of necessity. For example, Rossellini had to use on-location shooting for *Rome Open City* because the Cinecittà Studios were still occupied by war refugees. But by and large the "rough" neo-realist style was a well-planned reflection of both a serious social consciousness that wanted to tell the truth about an "Italy in rags", and an aesthetic ideal that turned "ugliness" into art. This combination produced several films of great power and beauty.

2. THE MAJOR NEO-REALIST DIRECTORS

Roberto Rossellini, Luchino Visconti and Vittorio De Sica are the most important directors of the neo-realist period. Each concentrated on a different aspect of the Italian scene and each developed his own particular film techniques, thereby broadening both the thematic and stylistic scope of neo-realism.

A. THE WAR: ROBERTO ROSSELLINI

Roberto Rossellini has been called the "father of neo-realism." He was born in Rome in 1906, and developed an early interest in politics, history and literature. Rossellini had his first directing experience doing short documentaries for L.U.C.E. in 1936 and then became well known in the early 1940's for his series of feature-length propaganda films. These include *La Nave Bianca* (*The Hospital Ship,* 1941), *Un Pilota Ritorna* (*A Pilot Returns,* 1942) *L'Uomo della croce* (*The Man of the Cross,* 1943). Despite the fact that these films were made for the regime Rossellini was no Fascist sympathizer. In fact during the resistance, Rossellini represented the Christian Democratic Party of the cinema branch of the CLN (Committee for National Liberation). Because Rossellini had extensive experience with documentary style films and because he had participated in the Resistance in Rome, he was the perfect candidate to make films about the war in Italy. Between 1945 and 1947, Rossellini directed three films about the war effort that are now collectively known as "The War Trilogy."

The first film of the War Trilogy is *Roma, Città Aperta* (*Rome Open City,* 1945). While Nazi troops were still occupying Rome in 1944 Rossellini had the idea of making a short film celebrating the courage of the Italian Resistance fighters. He began shooting the film almost immediately after Rome was liberated by the Allies. What was intended as a short film soon developed into a feature-length project.

Rome Open City deals with Rome in the last days of the Nazi occupation. The term "Open City" in diplomatic terminology refers to a city which in time of war has been declared by both sides to be free from all acts of military aggression. The title *Rome Open City* is, to say the least, ironic, for the film is testimony to the violence that marked the occupation period. The story involves the attempts of the Nazi occupation forces in Rome to find and execute the clandestine CLN members who have been carrying out guerrilla warfare against the Germans. The Italian partisans are involved in two struggles; one against the Nazis (and those Italian Fascists still loyal to them), the other against a severe shortage of food and other essential supplies. The film opens with documentary-style footage showing Nazi troops searching for Giorgio Manfredi, a Communist member of the CLN. (Manfredi, incidentally, was modelled after the real life Celeste Negarville, CLN hero who later became mayor of Turin). Manfredi, forced to remain in hiding, carries out his Resistance activity with the help of Don Pietro, a priest. But Manfredi's safety is

Cinema Nuovo

Roberto Rossellini's *Rome Open City* (1945).

19

threatened after he quarrels with his lover Marina, who has connections with the German Gestapo. Meanwhile, the children of the neighborhood where Manfredi is hiding, gamely form their own Resistance troop and are successful in bomb attacks against German positions. Everything is thrown into crisis when the Gestapo gets wind of Manfredi's whereabouts and makes a sweeping search of the neighborhood. The Gestapo manages to inflict serious losses in the CLN ranks, and the film ends without our witnessing the triumphant arrival of the Allied troops.

Rome Open City is by and large a story of defeat. To convey the full force of the defeat Rossellini boldly embraced a realist style, taking the cameras into the misery-stricken streets and homes of the capital. We witness wartime life in all its grimness, tragedy, and, at times, humor. Rossellini recreated the wartime suffering and tension so accurately that many viewers thought that they were actually seeing documentary footage. Not only did Rossellini use on-location shooting, he also employed a cast made up almost exclusively of non-professional actors (the exceptions were Aldo Fabrizi in the role of Don Pietro, and Anna Magnani as Pina, the fiancé of Manfredi's friend Francesco. Fabrizi and Magnani were former vaudeville performers who launched successful film careers with *Rome Open City*.) Many of the sequences of *Rome Open City* were improvised at the time of shooting. Rossellini also faced two severe material difficulties while trying to make his film: shortage of money and a lack of uniform film stock.

Hence without studios, without movie stars and without adequate money and supplies Rossellini made the film that inaugurated the neo-realist movement. The lack of conventional resources was a blessing in disguise, for without them Rossellini was better able to recreate reality in the bare terms that had been idealized by the *Cinema* group.

Despite being a story of defeat, *Rome Open City* allows a measure of optimism by presenting some positive themes. First of all Rossellini stresses the felicitous cooperation between seemingly unlikely allies such as the Communist Manfredi and the priest Don Pietro. The theme of solidarity and cooperation is a favorite one of Rossellini's, and the ideal of unity embodied in the partnership of Manfredi and Don Pietro can be seen as Rossellini's optimistic suggestion for an approach to Italy's post-war problems as well.

A second positive theme is the childrens' successful participation in the war effort. This activity is presented in terms of an initiation rite, an introduction to the harsh reality of political life gained by observing and imitating the courageous actions of the Resistance heroes. The last characters we see in the film are the children as they march down a hill whistling a partisan song. Out of the current defeat comes the hope that the childrens' cooperative struggle against injustice and oppression will have prepared them to carry their mentors' efforts to a positive conclusion in the rebuilding of Italy.

This combination of defeat and hope which is central to *Rome Open City* became a major element of neo-realist film. After *Rome Open City* there were few neo-realist films that did not temper the grim reality of suffering with a measure of hopeful anticipation.

In sum, Rossellini is considered the "father of neo-realism" because he inaugurated a type of film which looks unflinchingly at reality in all its grimness. He established the stylistic precedents of extensive on-location shooting, use of non-professional actors, and the rejection of rhetorical invention in favor of the quasi-documentary. Thematically, his sympathy for those who suffer, and his suggestion of hope for the future based on solidarity and compassion were ideas that all neo-realists adopted.

Rome Open City was the only major film to be made in Italy in 1945. It was highly acclaimed in Europe and the United States and it won the Grand Prize at the Cannes Film Festival in 1946.

In 1946 Rossellini made his second film about war, *Paisà*. The title comes from the term used by American G.I.s when referring to Italians, for *paesano* in Italian means, among other things, "comrade" (particularly in Southern Italy). *Paisà* is a collection of six episodes which trace the Northward movement of the Allied forces in Italy from 1943 and 1945. The episodes take place in, respectively, Sicily, Naples, Rome, Florence, the Apennine Mountains and the Po River Delta.

The Sicilian episode deals with the struggle for Sicily between the Nazi and Allied forces, and with the reaction of the native Sicilians to the American troops.

The Naples episode is about how the destitute Neapolitan children tried to steal from unwary American G.I.s. The final sequence in Naples is a haunting view of the cave dwellings of those who have been left homeless by the war.

In Rome Rossellini tells the story of an American soldier's romance with an Italian girl who is later forced by poverty into prostitution.

The Florence episode finds the Allies and Nazi troops separated by Florence's Arno River. The plot revolves around the attempt of an American nurse to get news about an Italian partisan she had once known who is presently leading the CLN attack behind enemy lines.

The fifth episode is a respite from the war. It involves the visit of three American chaplains, a Jew, a Catholic, and a Lutheran, to a monastery in the Apennine Mountains.

The sixth and final episode returns to warfare. It is about the hit-and-run type battle in the Po River Delta. The Allied and partisan forces face a better equipped German army and are defeated.

Thematically and stylistically *Paisà* is similar to *Rome Open City*. There are some important differences. *Paisà* is somewhat less optimistic than *Rome Open City*. Most of the episodes end in defeat with less emphasis placed on hope for the future. This is particularly evident in the role of the children who, rather than being symbols of hope are tragic victims of the military and economic consequences of warfare. Nevertheless the romances that occur in several episodes remind us that even in the midst of war, hope survives in the strength of human emotions.

Furthermore, the fact that *Paisà* is a collection of separate episodes allows a greater complexity of characterization and point of view. For instance, rather than the single opposition of good and evil (Partisans vs. Nazis) that we find in *Rome Open City,* in *Paisà* a new force, the American army, is introduced and portrayed in more ambiguous terms. The Americans are usually generous and good-willed, but because of their lack of understanding of foreign cultures they are at times insensitive to the fears and anxieties of the war-weary Italian population.

Finally, in focusing on the war and foreign occupation in different regions of Italy (rather than just one city) *Paisà* introduces a historical dimension by recalling Italy's long foreign domination prior to the unification of 1870.

In sum, *Paisà* represents a step forward in the neo-realist development of Rossellini because it introduces ambiguity and complexity of characterization and point of view. It expands the documentary tendency of realist film by including a larger historical dimension.

The third film of Rossellini's War Trilogy is entitled *Germania Anno Zero* (*Germany in the Year Zero*, 1947). This is the least successful film of the trilogy. *Germany in the Year Zero* explores the causes of the rise of Nazism. It was filmed in Berlin and centers on a thirteen-year old child, Edmund, who undergoes a series of symbolic and frightening encounters with family members and acquaintances. These encounters culminate in Edmund's suicide, and Edmund's tragedy is to be seen as the tragedy of Nazi Germany. The emphasis on symbolism is a departure from Rossellini's two earlier war films. Another difference is the psychological theme, prevalent in the portrayal of the child Edmund. Whereas the children in *Rome Open City* and *Paisà* are seen exclusively with respect to their reaction to social reality, in *Germany in the Year Zero* we are invited to explore the workings of Edmund's mind. On the other hand, *Germania Anno Zero* resembles *Paisà* in its exploration of historical phenomena.

Rossellini and his War Trilogy inaugurated the neo-realist movement. Although later neo-realist directors concentrated on different subjects (war was not the dominant theme in neo-realism) they adopted the major aspects of Rossellini's foundation: a bold, realistic recreation of suffering and poverty, partly mitigated by a *hopeful look for future change*. The stylistic elements that Rossellini used (on-location shooting in often grim surroundings, rejection of rhetorical invention, use of non-professional actors and a reliance on improvisation) were all to become characteristic of neo-realism in general.

B. THE LAND: LUCHINO VISCONTI

We have already mentioned Luchino Visconti as the director of *Ossessione* (1942), which was at that time the most notable practical expression of the realist theories of the *Cinema* group. In 1948 Visconti turned his attention to the problems of Italy's rural poor. The result was the film that some consider the finest of the neo-realist period: *La Terra trema (The Earth Trembles)*.

Visconti was born into the Milanese aristocracy in 1906. The Visconti name stands alongside other great ruling families in Italian history such as Della Scala, Medici and Sforza. Luchino enthusiastically developed several of the cultural interests that his family was known for, particularly theater and opera. Before long, Visconti was attracted to film and in 1936 travelled to France to assist Jean Renoir in *Les Bas-fonds (The Underworld)* and *Une Partie de Campagne (A Day in the Country)*.

Visconti returned to Italy a year later and joined the *Cinema* group. He directed several plays and then made *Ossessione* in 1942. During the war he was active in the Resistance and was eventually captured and imprisoned in Rome by the Nazis who planned to execute him. Visconti was an object of concern to the Nazis not only because of his Resistance activity, but also because the film *Ossessione* had earned him a reputation as a subversive. Visconti managed to escape from prison just before the American Fifth Army entered Rome in 1944. Hence, Visconti actually lived through that period that Rossellini depicted in *Rome Open City*.

After the war Visconti returned to his theater productions in Rome. At the same time, his interests continued to focus on two key figures who were to influence him in the film *La Terra trema:* the novelist Giovanni Verga and the Communist thinker Antonio Gramsci (see Chapter II). Visconti originally intended to make a trilogy about the Sicilian peasantry: one part each for fishing, mining and agriculture. *La Terra trema,* the epic-length episode on fishing, is the only one that was completed. The story is based on Verga's novel *I Malavoglia* (the literal translation of the title would be "The Malavoglia Family" but the English translator of the novel has chosen instead *The House by the Medlar Tree*). *I Malavoglia,* which takes place in the Sicilian coastal village of Aci Trezza, is about a young fisherman Antonio Malavoglia who tries to raise his family out of poverty by singlehandedly fighting the exploitative owners of the village fishing boats. These owners employ all of the village fishermen for barely sustenance wages and Antonio decides to take out a loan with the family house as collateral in order to buy his own boat. The project ends in failure largely because Antonio is unable to enlist the support of the other fishermen in Aci Trezza.

Visconti in his film is very faithful to Verga's story (he simply changes the Malavoglia family name to Valastro). More importantly he is faithful to Verga's realistic portrayal of the Sicilian poor, showing their fundamental passions, their superstitions, their basic stoic nobility, which often involves a passive acceptance of the vicissitudes of fate. Visconti, influenced by Verga's attempt to accurately reproduce the speech of the Sicilian peasants, employed an entirely non-professional cast and had them speak their own Sicilian dialect (which incidentally is so different from standard Italian that when *La Terra trema* was released in Italy, occasional commentary was needed during the film to help non-Sicilians follow the story).

Visconti is very concerned with showing us the strength and nobility of bearing of the fishermen of Aci Trezza and to do so he makes extensive use of close-ups, something rare in Rossellini films. Visconti takes pains to show us the day to day, even banal activities of his subjects, another departure from Rossellini and his predilection for extraordinary political or military situations. Like Rossellini, Visconti employs a documentary style, but in a different way. Rossellini's films, by concentrating on political and military crises often look like newsreels. *La Terra trema,* on the other hand, in its patient study of the daily habits of the fishermen and their families is similar, at times, to a good National Geographic Film report.

The most important change that Visconti makes in *La Terra trema* is that in portraying Antonio Valastro's struggle against the fishermen he emphasizes the idea of class struggle. In doing so, Visconti is more of a Gramscian than a Marxist (See Chapter II) for he is concentrating on a rural rather than an industrial situation, and pays close attention to the regional question by emphasizing the particularly Sicilian manners, ways of thinking, speech, and physical appearance. According to Gramsci (and Visconti) all of these rural factors must be carefully evaluated if a class struggle is to result in significant change. *La Terra trema* is a convincing portrayal of a social struggle that fails to result in any significant change. Nevertheless, at the end of the film it is evident that despite his defeat, Antonio is still determined to overcome the exploitation in his village.

In sum, Luchino Visconti in *La Terra trema* shifts the emphasis from the war to post-war problems of a rural population. Visconti does many things differently than Rossellini: he "studies" his characters more, he is concerned with their mundane activity as a means of knowing what they are like. There are fewer political "events" in Visconti, but on the other hand, Visconti's political ideology is much clearer than Rossellini's.

Stylistically *La Terra trema* moves more slowly than Rossellini's films. There is less emphasis on action and more emphasis on character development. Hence, there are many long sequences that may at first viewing seem "unnecessary" for the development of the plot, but which are actually crucial to Visconti's patient study of the daily life in Aci Trezza. Visconti's long sequences succeed in making the audience live with the characters. Life moves slowly in Aci Trezza, and Visconti makes us feel that slow pace.

Despite their different approaches, Visconti and Rossellini shared the compassionate identification with their characters' plight and both directors avoided a pessimistic view of the future. Furthermore, the realist ideal of "letting the facts speak for themselves" was successfully attained by Rossellini and Visconti. The vow of the *Cinema* group to transfer the style of Verga to the screen was evidently no hollow promise.

C. THE CITY: VITTORIO DE SICA

The third major neo-realist director, and one of the most prolific directors in the history of Italian film, was Vittorio De Sica. De Sica was born and raised in Naples. He acted in stage musicals and vaudeville and in 1932 made his film-acting debut in Mario Camerini's comedy *Men What Scoundrels!* (1932). By 1940, De Sica's renown as a comic actor was rivalled by few. In

1940 he began directing film comedies and then in 1943 he made *The Children Are Watching Us,* one of the films that looked ahead to neo-realism (see Chapter III). Collaborating with De Sica on *The Children Are Watching Us* was the noted theorist and scriptwriter Cesare Zavattini.

Zavattini laid a great part of the theoretical foundation of neo-realism. He insisted that directors should reject dramatic conventions of plot and suspense and concentrate on life as it appears day in and day out. Zavattini felt that the best way for audiences to get to know, and hence to identify with others was not by watching them in unusual, "eventful" situations but in the routine of their daily lives. He once said that the ideal film would be ninety minutes in the life of a man in which nothing happened. A more accurate summary of Zavattini's neo-realist ideal is the following:

> There are the others . . . the others . . . the others are important . . . that is the most important thing. . . . The men who live around us, what do they do, how do they live, are they well, do they suffer, and why are they ill, why do they suffer? . . . Everything that happens around us, often even the most banal things seen on the street, besides the most serious events whether they be far or near, has a significance, a human, social and dramatic meaning and raises great problems. Problems which are ours too, since nothing which happens around us is foreign to us, to the extent that we are men, a part of humanity. Here are my fascinating, inexhaustible fundamental sources—sources of inspiration, meditation and creative action, and they ought to be so for everyone in the cinema too.[7]

Zavattini was a scriptwriter for over 100 Italian films, but it was through his collaboration with De Sica that his international reputation was made. He assisted De Sica in all of his neo-realist films. The friendship and collaboration of De Sica and Zavattini rivalled the French team of Marcel Carné and Jacques Prevert.

In *The Children Are Watching Us* Zavattini pushed De Sica to combine his comic instincts with a hard-core investigation beneath the façade of the Fascist ideal of the Italian family. De Sica's comedy had always had a very human, sympathetic tone and under Zavattini's influence he developed a realist style which, while often grim and unpleasant was at the same time the warmest and most emotional of the three major neo-realist directors.

Together De Sica and Zavattini made four neo-realist films between 1946 and 1952. All four dealt with the metropolis and all have become classics. The first was *Sciuscià* (*Shoeshine,* 1946). *Shoeshine* is the tragic story of two young shoeshine boys in Rome who unknowingly become involved in the black market and are caught and imprisoned. The film is a comment on the callousness of the system of justice and the horrors of the juvenile prison system. Using the two small boys as protagonists allows De Sica to contrast youthful innocence with the corruption of the adult world. The boys' dream of escaping poverty in the beginning of the film is represented by a horse which they manage to buy after pooling their meagre resources. The moments of exhilaration that they share in riding the horse through the park are suddenly obliterated by the frightening series of events that follow their "crime".

In *Ladri di biciclette* (*Bicycle Thieves,* 1948), very loosely adapted from a novel by Luigi Bartolini, De Sica and Zavattini show how adults as well as children can be innocent victims of an insensitive system. The social background of *Bicycle Thieves* is the severe unemployment of post-war Italy. Antonio Ricci, who has not had a job in two years finally finds work as a bill poster, a job that requires a bicycle. On Antonio's first day of work, his bicycle is stolen and he faces the loss of his job. With his young son Bruno, Antonio spends an entire weekend searching for his bicycle in the streets and squares of Rome. This search not only gives a vividly accurate view of post-war Rome, it also gradually builds within the audience the despair that Antonio feels as he fails to recover his source of livelihood. One of the most frustrating aspects of Antonio's plight is that he is relatively alone in his search. The police are unsympathetic, as is a local union hall. Once again, as in *Shoeshine,* the insensitivity of institutions comes under attack. While Antonio is at the police station a journalist asks if there is anything worth reporting. The officer answers, "No, just a stolen bicycle." While De Sica may adopt a quasi-documentary style he obviously does not agree with what journalism considers newsworthy. De Sica and Zavattini want to show that there can be tragedy in even the most insignificant events.

The third neo-realist film of De Sica and Zavattini is *Miracolo a Milano* (*Miracle in Milan,* 1951). *Miracle in Milan* is a story about vagabonds and homeless families who live in the outskirts of Milan, Italy's largest industrial center. It is one of the few neo-realist films that portray rich people. The purpose, of course, is to heighten the contrast between rich and poor. One of the most memorable sequences in the film is one in which the slum dwellers stand by the train tracks watching a deluxe train pass slowly by filled with the well-to-do. The story develops into a struggle between the slum dwellers, who have managed to build modest homes on a vacant lot, and a group of scheming developers who wish to expropriate the land for their own profit.

In *Miracle in Milan* De Sica gives a free hand to his comic tendencies. In fact the cast includes the famous Neopolitan comic actor Totò who plays the happy-go-lucky leader of the slum-dwellers. There are also several sequences that incorporate dreams, fantasies, visions and even ghosts. Because of the comedy and fantasy, many critics hesitate to call *Miracle in Milan* a

Cinema Nuovo

Vittorio De Sica's *Bicycle Thieves* (1948).

neo-realist film. Nevertheless De Sica's portrayal of extreme poverty in contrast with the wealth of Northern Italy, and his identification with the cause of the slum dwellers are certainly within the reformist spirit of neo-realism.

In 1952 De Sica and Zavattini made what is generally considered to be the last film of the neo-realist period: *Umberto D. Umberto D* takes place in Rome and is the story of a retired government employee named Umberto (played by the famous linguistics professor Carlo Battisti). Umberto struggles to live on a pension that is not adequate to pay for his rent and food. The film begins with a protest march of retired persons which is callously broken up by the police. This opening sequence signals a return to the De Sica attack on institutional insensitivity that marked his first two neo-realist films. What is different about *Umberto D* is that it deals not with people born and raised in abject poverty, but with a formerly middle class man struggling not only to pay his expenses but to maintain his former demeanor as a white collar official. His landlady is anxious to throw him out of his room so that she can remodel, and out of despair Umberto feigns sickness in order to enter a state hospital and be fed for a few days. Umberto's solitude is underlined by the fact that his only friend is his small dog. Umberto's poverty and isolation finally lead him to contemplate suicide.

De Sica differs from Rossellini and Visconti by avoiding "major events" on the one hand and political ideology on the other. By and large De Sica is concerned with how injustice effects the daily lives of its victims. Insensitivity is the main villain in De Sica's films, not war or exploitation of one class by another, although the latter is by no means completely absent. The emphasis on insensitivity is closely tied to the metropolitan setting of De Sica's films, for the type of insensitivity which De Sica attacks is generally of an institutional or bureaucratic nature.

De Sica also likes to occasionally accentuate the minor human imperfections of his characters. The result is that audiences probably identify more emotionally with them than they do with the characters of other neo-realist directors. The compassion that De Sica invites from the audience is a key aspect of his hope for reform for it is precisely this commiseration that can break the cold insensitivity that often afflicts the big city.

The three major neo-realist directors concentrated on different settings and themes, and developed their particular interests with different techniques. Because of this, neo-realism was not a narrow school but one that could expand to deal with any type of social injustice. What joined the three directors was their desire to identify with those who suffer, to do so in realistic terms, and to show where, despite all the grimness, hope was warranted. All in all this realism was a call to action, for to repeat Zavattini's words, "To depict poverty is to protest against it."

3. MINOR NEO-REALIST DIRECTORS

Besides Rossellini, Visconti and De Sica there were several other directors who made neo-realist films. They are not well known in the United States but are very familiar to Italian audiences. Alberto Lattuada, Pietro Germi, Giuseppe De Santis, Carlo Lizzani, Luigi Zampa and *Renato Castellani* are the most noteworthy of these "minor" neo-realist directors.

Alberto Lattuada, whose "manifesto of neo-realism" was cited above helped organize the dramatic and controversial Milan Triennale in 1940. Lattuada was born in Milan in 1914. He became an architect and then in 1940 was one of the founders of the *Cineteca Italiana* in Milan. A year later he was in Rome. His first experience in a film was as a scriptwriter for Mario Soldati's *Piccolo Mondo Antico* (*Little Old Fashioned World*, 1941). Before long Lattuada was firmly within the neo-realist school and his films boldly portray the violence that marked the last days of the war. *Il bandito* (*The Bandit*, 1946) is about an Italian prisoner of war who returns home finding his family members either dead or missing. *Senza Pietà* (*Without Pity*, 1948) is about an American G.I. who falls in love with an Italian prostitute and tries to rescue her from the exploitative trap into which poverty has driven her. *Il Mulino del Po* (*The Mill on the Po*, 1949), based on the novel by Riccardo Bacchelli, deals with peasant unrest in Italy in 1876 and helped expand the concept of neo-realism by showing that it could be directly applied to past and not just contemporary settings. This was to be important when neo-realism was revived in later years. *The Mill on the Po* is considered by many to be Lattuada's finest film. Lattuada went on to make films in several genres (including the love story *Stay As You Are*, released in the United States in 1980).

If Lattuada was similar to Rossellini in portraying the effects of war, Pietro Germi resembled Visconti in his concern for Sicilian peasants. Born in the Liguria region of Italy in 1914, Germi studied at the C.S.C. He directed several neo-realist films and acted in two of them. He is best known for *In nome della legge* (*In the Name of the Law*, 1948) where he uncovers Mafia corruption in Sicily. *Il cammino della speranza* (*The Road of Hope*, 1950) is about Sicilians who emigrate to France in search of work. Like Lattuada, Germi was well versed in other genres. He excelled in comedy, as is evident in *Divorzio all'Italiana* (*Divorce Italian Style*, 1961).

Cinema Nuovo

Pietro Germi's *Il cammino della speranza* (1950).

27

Another director concerned with the peasantry was Giuseppe De Santis, who was part of the *Cinema* group and a student of C.S.C. He was a scriptwriter for *Ossessione* and then made a trilogy about the peasantry: *Caccia Tragica* (*Pursuit*, 1947), *Riso Amaro* (*Bitter Rice*, 1948) and *Non c'è pace tra gli ulivi* (*No Peace Among the Olives*, 1949).

Carlo Lizzani, born in Rome in 1922, has had a diversified film career including contributions to *Bianco e Nero* and *Cinema*, and serving as assistant in dozens of films. He also directed several documentaries. His best known neo-realist film, *Achtung Banditi!* (1951) is about the Resistance in Genoa, but it was released too late to gain a following. Lizzani is also well known for his history of Italian film *Il Cinema Italiano* (1953).

Finally in the later stages of the neo-realist period there were some films that attempted to mix neo-realism and comedy. These earned the nickname "rosy neo-realism". Luigi Zampa directed a riotous attack on the absurdity of war called *Vivere in pace* (*To Live in Peace*, 1946). Renato Castellani directed three very popular films injecting sentimental comedy into the neo-realist portrayal of poverty: *Sotto il Sole di Roma* (*In the Sunshine of Rome*, 1947), *È Primavera* (*Springtime*, 1949) and *Due Soldi di Speranza* (*Two Pennyworth of Hope*, 1952).

Despite its popularity "rosy neo-realism" was attacked by some critics who felt that it strayed too far from the neo-realist style.

V. THE DECLINE
OF NEO-REALISM

As stated in Chapter IV, most critics consider *Umberto D* (1952) to be the last film of the neo-realist era. Why did neo-realism decline at this time? It was mostly because of the political and economic situation. First of all it must be pointed out that neo-realist films, even though they were acclaimed internationally were not very popular in Italy itself. *Rome Open City* is a rare exception. It is not difficult to understand why Italians did not flock to see neo-realist films: the grim social reality was so close at hand that for most Italians it seemed senseless to view it on film. In harsh times people usually prefer escape-films, many of which were released in Italy in this period.

A corollary of the lack of popularity of neo-realism in Italy at that time was the lack of funds for production. In 1948 only 54 films were made in Italy. Eight hundred seventy-four films were imported (668 from the United States). Only 13% of box office receipts went to Italian film-makers. A depressed film industry is a vicious circle: low production brings in little money which in turn decreases production. Neo-realist directors suffered greatly from this situation and turned to the government for help. But the political situation had changed since the promising 1945 coalition government of Christian Democrats, Socialists, Communists and Republicans.

In May of 1947, Prime Minister De Gasperi felt confident enough to establish a government comprised of only the Christian Democrats and a few independents. In December he expanded this government to include two smaller moderate parties, but the significant fact was the ousting of the Socialists and the Communists. De Gasperi's maneuvering set the stage for the elections of April 18, 1949. The Christian Democrats (supported by the United States) tried to represent the elections as a choice between capitalism and communism in accordance with the cold war mentality that was developing in the West. The result was a significant victory for the Christian Democrats who received 48.5% of the vote compared with a combined total of 31% for the Socialists and Communists (who had temporarily allied themselves as the "Popular Democratic Front"). As a result De Gasperi formed a government dominated by Christian Democrats but including representatives of the small moderate parties. The Socialists and Communists went into opposition.

All in all of course these events signalled a shift to the right in Italian politics. The result was discouragement among those who had hoped for sweeping social change. The postwar optimism among reformists was already dimmed.

Among those who were disappointed were the neo-realist film directors. Nevertheless they continued to press the government for financial assistance. Assistance arrived in 1949 but under certain conditions. The government agreed to partial subsidation of Italian film production but the amounts of the subsidies were dependent on the "artistic and technical merits" of the films, to be determined by government officials. The arrangement became known as the "Andreotti law" (named after the cabinet minister Giulio Andreotti, recently Prime Minister of Italy). The Government had been overtly critical of neo-realism because of its grim portrayal of Italian society and therefore questioned its "artistic and technical merits."

29

The meagre subsidies for neo-realist films in subsequent years reflected this judgement. In Andreotti's words "If it is true that evil can be fought by harshly spotlighting its most miserable aspects, it is also true that De Sica has rendered bad service to his country if people throughout the world start thinking that Italy in the 20th century is the same as *Umberto D.*"[8]

Another probable cause for the decline of neo-realism was Italy's economy: it was entering its famous "take off" period, often called Italy's "economic miracle." The dramatic rise in gross national product, aided by the Marshall Plan, made the problems of Italy's poor less visible if not less serious.

The new prosperity was reflected in the subject matter of the films of the 1950's. Many directors, Rossellini included, became interested in how the well-to-do often sacrificed fundamental human values such as love and friendship in exchange for a comfortable economic status.

Zavattini, however, was bitterly disappointed over the failure of the directors of the neo-realist period to continue their depiction of poverty. He refused to accept the changed political situation, the new prosperity, or the tastes of the Italian audiences as excuses for neo-realism's decline. "It is not neo-realism that has fallen," he said "but the courage to be a neo-realist."

VI. REVIVALS OF NEO-REALISM

The term neo-realism can be used in two senses. In the restricted sense it refers to the realistic style of films that were made in Italy from 1945–1952. In a broader sense the term neo-realism is also applied to later films that tried to revive the neo-realist style.

Just as the rise of neo-realism in 1945 and its decline in 1952 reflect the contemporary political and economic situation in Italy, so the beginning of the revival of neo-realism is a barometer of politics and the economy. In the late 1950's and early 1960's the Christian Democratic Party began to relax its *laissez faire* economic policies and Italy began a slow but steady move towards the left. This shift was also reflected in the gradual increase in support for the Italian Communist Party. It is not surprising then, that Roberto Rossellini's return to neo-realism with *Il Generale Della Rovere* (1959) and *Era Notte a Roma* (1960) should occur at this time.

De Sica was not far behind. He played the lead in *Il Generale Della Rovere* and then collaborated with Zavattini to make *La Ciociara* (*Two Women*, 1960) based on the novel by Alberto Moravia. Two of De Sica's best known films in the United States were also revivals of neo-realism: *Il Giardino dei Finzi-Contini* (The Garden of the Finzi-Contini, 1970) and *Una Breve vacanza* (A Brief Vacation, 1973).

A younger director, Ermanno Olmi (born in 1931) made neo-realist style films such as *Il Tempo si è fermato* (*Time Stopped*, 1959), *Il Posto* (*The Place*, 1961) and *I Fidanzati* (*The Betrothed*, 1963) all of which show the influence of De Sica. Olmi's most recent film *L'Albero degli zoccoli* (*Tree of the Wooden Clogs*, 1979) is a beautiful re-evocation of the neo-realist studies of Italian peasantry.

Ettore Scola, another younger director, made a film entitled *C'eravamo tanto amati* (*We All Loved Each Other So Much*, 1977) which is a tribute to the original neo-realists, and his recent film *Una Giornata particolare* (*A Special Day*, 1977) is deliberately in the style of De Sica, to whom the film is dedicated.

Another recent neo-realist film that deserves mention is Francesco Rosi's *Cristo si è fermato a Eboli* (*Christ Stopped at Eboli*, 1979), based on Carlo Levi's outstanding novel (see Ch. I).

Of these revivals of neo-realism some portray contemporary settings *(A Brief Vacation)* while others go back in history (*A Special Day* for instance reveals the zenith of Mussolini's power while *The Tree of the Wooden Clogs* takes place at the turn of the century).

The rich diversity of subject matter and settings of the recent neo-realist films demonstrates that neo-realism is anything but a moribund movement. It has proven to be adaptable to a wide range of political, historical, social and economic subjects, while maintaining its essential "fundamental humanism". It does not suffice to say that neo-realism is simply a study of the social problems of post-war Italy. Neo-realism is above all a way of looking at reality, and that perspective of reality is still vibrant.

VII. BRIEF SURVEY OF ITALIAN HISTORY 1947-1960

1. POST WAR ITALY

Even after the Unification of Italy in 1870, it was soon evident that the "Risorgimento" (the "resurgence", Italy's 19th century unification movement) had not eradicated the deep regional loyalties that made many citizens feel more "Venetian" or "Roman" or "Neopolitan" than "Italian". The Risorgimento was largely the work of an elite group of politicians, diplomats, lawyers and intellectuals which left the masses indifferent. Some of the patriots themselves were aware of this. One of them, Massimo D'Azeglio, proclaimed "We have made Italy; we must now make Italians".[9]

With the arrival of Mussolini and Fascism in 1922, the creation of a national consciousness and patriotism became a kind of state religion. Mussolini portrayed himself as the heir to the Risorgimento tradition and he set out to equate nationalism with militarism and adventures of conquest in Africa. Mussolini alienated those who viewed the Risorgimento tradition as essentially a liberal one involving increasing popular participation in the political process, free speech and peaceful co-existence with European nations of a like cultural tradition. The irony of Mussolini's mission to secure for Italy "a place in the sun" was that in the end he left Italy more vulnerable to foreign powers than it had been for centuries. The Franco-Spanish struggle for hegemony in 16th century Italy, the Napoleonic invasions, the Austrian sovereignty over Northern and Central Italy in the 19th century, all of these seem mild when compared to the bitter struggle fought with modern weapons in World War II between the Nazis and the Anglo-Americans, a two year conflict which moved from Sicily to the Alps and left thousands of Italians dead and many more homeless.

As the war drew to a close the United States found itself in an unusual position: it was the occupying power in Italy, the most recent in a long list of foreign invaders, a situation made more tense because of the large numbers of Italian-Americans in the States who considered themselves patriotic Americans yet who wished the American occupation forces to be lenient in their treatment of Italy. Most problematic was the relationship between the Anglo-American troops and the underground Italian "partisan" units which had assisted the allies in their fight against the Nazis. While the allies appreciated the courageous collaboration of the Italian partisans they were concerned about the large number of Communists and Socialists that made up the partisan military and political organizations. The Allies knew that the Italian Communists and Socialists wished to transform their leadership role in the anti-Nazi resistance to a much broader political role in post-war Italy. As one American colonel said as he watched a large partisan unit march by in a victory parade "It is beautiful and moving, and frightening as well." The ambivalence of the Americans toward the partisans gradually became transmuted into pure distrust during the early post-war period as the Cold War between the United States and the Soviet Union caused the U.S. to resist any attempts of Western European leftists to expand their influence. It is in this regard that Italian politics remained for the time being subject to foreign influence. Because of the enormous destruction suffered during the war Italy was in desperate need of economic aid, and the United States used economic assistance to persuade the Italian Christian Democratic party to reduce Communist and Socialist participation in important decision-making positions.[10]

American policy was facilitated by the presence of a highly skilled Christian Democratic Prime Minister Alcide De Gasperi who along with Charles De Gaulle in France and Konrad Adenauer in Germany helped to give Western Europe stability after five years of war. Italy gained some concrete benefits from De Gasperi's leadership and American aid. By 1949 economic production had reached pre-war levels and the ground was laid for Italy's famous "economic boom" of the 1950s. Italy was re-integrated into the European community after the hiatus of the Fascist period and World War II. But a price was paid as well. Italy's economic recovery touched a small percentage of the population; large sectors were extremely poor and seemed to have little representation in the government. The Communists and Socialists who appealed to the politically and economically disenfranchised ploddingly built up their organizations and looked to a future when they would have more influence. Meanwhile the hope of many Italians that their country might become part of a European "third force" between the superpowers was disappointed by the increasing division of the world into two blocks and the creation of the North Atlantic Treaty Organization in 1949.

2. ITALIAN POLITICAL PARTIES

Before continuing our survey of post-war Italian politics it will be useful to pause for a moment to outline the major Italian political parties. This is essential to an understanding of Italian politics because political parties in Italy (as in most European countries) have much greater influence than their American counterparts.

The Italian government is based on a parliamentary, not a presidential system. In a parliamentary system the prime minister and his cabinet must maintain the support of the legislature to remain in power. A vote of no confidence by the legislature may result in the fall of the government (in a parliamentary system the term government is used synonomously with "cabinet") and possibly new elections. This close tie between the executive and legislative branches contrast with the presidential system (e.g. that of the United States) in which no measure of acrimony between the legislative and executive branches (short of impeachment) can bring down a president. The British parliamentary system is fairly simple because until recently there were only two major parties (a third is currently gaining strength). But in Italy the party rivalries are complex because there are presently eight major parties which are represented in the parliament, which is divided into a Senate and a Chamber of Deputies. Whereas in British parliamentary elections one party may be counted on to gain over 50% of the seats in parliament and thus to have the right to name the prime minister and the cabinet, in Italy no party in the post-war period has ever topped 50%, so Italian cabinets are either coalitions of more than one party, or are based on one party with the agreement that other parties will support its proposals in the legislature. This complexity is the source of the rapid rise and fall of Italian cabinets.

The largest party in every election since the war has been the *Christian Democratic Party* (Democrazia Cristiana—DC) which is the heir of the old Popular Party founded in 1919 by Don Luigi Sturzo, a Sicilian priest. Ever since Alcide De Gasperi succeeded Ferruccio Parri (the leftist leader of the brief partisan-led cabinet) in 1946, the Christian Democrats have maintained ascendancy in the Italian Parliament. Ideologically the DC is a centrist party but it has both conservative and leftist wings.

The second largest party is the *Italian Communist Party* (Partito Comunista Italiano—PCI) which was formed by a splinter group of the older Italian Socialist Party in 1921. One of its founders, Antonio Gramsci (1891–1937) has been its key source of ideology and an important philosophical factor in the party's considerable independence from the Soviet Union. The party maintains strong support among workers, but its increasing moderation on such issues as nationalization and land reform have won over many middle class voters. The PCI is strongest in the "industrial triangle" (Milan—Turin—Genoa) and in the central regions of Emilia-Romagna, Tuscany and Umbria, the so-called "red-belt". While no communists have been in the cabinet since 1947 several local governments including most major cities are under PCI leadership.

The *Italian Socialist Party* (Partito Socialista Italiano—PSI) was founded in 1892 by the popular Filippo Turati and has been repeatedly beset by factional quarrels and secessions. It has allied itself at times with the Communists (in the 1940s and early 1950s) and with the Christian Democrats (intermittently in the 1960s and 1970s) and has often been accused of lack of direction. Because of its flexibility and size (third largest party) the PSI is crucial in the cabinet-jockeying which characterizes Italian politics.

The *Italian Social Democratic Party* (Partito Socialista Democratico Italiano—PSDI) was formed in 1952 by Giuseppe Saragat from a coalition of centrist groups within the PSI. The PSDI is considerably smaller than the PSI and is opposed to collaboration with the Communists. Between 1966 and 1969 the PSI and PSDI were reunited.

The *Italian Republican Party* (Partito Repubblicano Italiano—PRI) is a small moderate leftist party which since the war has strongly supported a pro-Western position and membership in NATO. The adoption of these stands by the PSI and PCI has undercut some PRI support.

The *Italian Liberal Party* (Partito Liberale Italiano—PLI) was founded in 1848 by the major architect of Italian unification Count Camillo di Cavour. The PLI is a conservative party which supports free enterprise capitalism and draws most of its limited support from businessmen (most of whom favor the DC).

Americans are occasionally mislead by the terms "republican" (as in the PRI) and "liberal" (PLI) in Italian party nomenclature. In Italy both terms conserve their 19th century meanings in which republican meant in favor of a republic and opposed to a monarchy; liberal meant in favor of *laissez-faire* capitalism. Thus contrary to the American definitions an Italian Republican is on the left and a liberal is on the right.

On the extreme right is the *Italian Social Movement* (Movimento Sociale Italiano—MSI). The MSI, led by Giorgio Almirante, is a neo-Fascist party which has two faces: a "respectable" parliamentary one and an unofficial violent side which supports rightist terrorist activity.

The *Radical Party* (Partito Radicale—PR) first gained parliamentary representation in 1976. Led by Marco Panella the PR is a small but growing party which concentrates on social issues such as abortion, women's rights, the environment and nuclear policy. Its support comes from progressive elements of the middle class.

One may for the sake of clarity arrange the Italian political parties from left to right in the following manner, keeping in mind that all parties have factions that do not strictly follow the party line and may overlap with other parties on certain issues. The Radical Party is not included because it has as yet not produced a comprehensive ideology and prefers instead to address single issues.

```
L                                                                      R
E                                                                      I
F      PCI      PSI      PSDI      PRI      DC      PLI      MSI        G
T                                                                      H
                                                                       T
```

3. THE FIFTIES

Between 1948 and 1952 Italy was governed by "centrist" cabinets (DC, PLI, PRI, PSDI) led by DC's De Gasperi. By 1952 it began to appear that a centrist majority might not survive the next parliamentary elections, scheduled for 1953. The Christian Democrats thus decided to tamper with the election laws, passing a measure calling for any party that polled over 50% of the popular vote to receive two-thirds of the seats in the Chamber of Deputies. The DC was hoping for an improvement of its impressive 1948 vote tally. The new measure, dubbed the "legge truffa" (swindle law) backfired, for the DC gained only 40% of the vote. De Gasperi was unable to re-suscitate the old four-party coalition and retired from politics. He died a year later.

The De Gasperi era having been closed, the Christian Democrats continued to construct centrist coalitions under the leadership of Marco Scelba and Antonio Segni. But by now one of De Gasperi's failings began to haunt the DC: the veteran prime minister had neglected the grass roots organization of his party, preferring to depend on the help of local Catholic Church parishes to mobilize support for Christian Democratic candidates. The DC had reached stagnation as a party while others, especially the Communist Party, were working hard to construct efficient party machines. Recognizing this weakness in his party Amintore Fanfani organized a new current in the DC entitled Democratic Initiative which sought to broaden the DC constituency by appealing to the popular masses. Fanfani, an economics professor, was concerned about the abuses of free enterprise capitalism and the DC's identification with it. He felt that the DC could only prevent a leftist takeover in Italy by supporting moderate social reform and controls on major industries. Fanfani was an important influence in the DC's cautious move toward the left in the later 1950s.

For the time being social reform took a back seat to parliamentary and cabinet infighting, and the legislature that served from 1953 to 1958 became known as the "legislature of immobilism". Despite the fact that problems of housing, unemployment, underdevelopment showed little sign of amelioration they ceased to have the hold on the public consciousness during the mid 1950s. Even students seemed more concerned with careers than social issues. It was not difficult for many Italians to ignore the darker side of the economic picture because the growth of Italy's gross national income was one of the highest in Europe in the 1950s. This reflected the partial success of the Vanoni Plan of 1955, a long-term development strategy which aimed to couple economic growth with the elimination of unemployment and a closing of the enormous "prosperity gap" between Northern and Southern Italy. The failure of the latter two objectives invited increasing pressure from the left. At the same time, however, there was a resurgence of right-wing political activity. Officials of the Fascist regime had never been adequately persecuted and many now offered their support to the MSI, the PLI and the small but vocal monarchists who longed for a return of the king.

The conservative atmosphere of the fifties was encouraged by certain factions in the Vatican. The Church had been awarded special privileges in the famous Lateran Accords signed with the Fascists in 1929 and many prelates were determined that the Church exert a powerful influence in temporal affairs in post-war Italy as well. While De Gasperi was Prime Minister he had resisted overt clericalism but after his death conservatives in the Vatican became bolder, particularly because Pope Pius XII had become ill and was not able to control his subordinates effectively.

Foremost among the right wing cardinals was Alfredo Ottaviani who used the lay organization Catholic Action as a weapon in his crusade of censorship, anti-communism, and restriction of civil liberties. In this effort he had the full support of Catholic Action's President, Luigi Gedda. Ottaviani and Gedda effectively reversed Catholic Action's role during the Fascist period when it was supported by Pius XI as a bulwark against Fascist indoctrination of Italian youth. Cardinal Ottaviani also helped to repress the famous worker-priest movement in France, which had been an attempt to identify the lower clergy with French industrial workers. This too reversed the policy of Pius XI who in the 1930s had been interested in the democratic socialist ideas of the French Catholic thinkers Emmanuel Mounier and Jacques Maritain. In the 1930s many Catholics had hoped for a rapprochement with the humanitarian economic ideals of socialism and the civil liberties of democracy. The increasing influence of conservatives in the Vatican in the 1950s temporarily dimmed this hope.

In foreign affairs two major occurrences had important effects in Italy. First of all by the mid 1950s the Cold War had begun to ease up. This encouraged the Italian Socialists and Communists to look favorably upon Italy's ties with Western Europe, such as the NATO alliance. Secondly, Nikita Krushchev's famous 1956 speech revealing the crimes of the Stalin era spurred the PCI and the PSI to distance themselves from the Soviet Union's Communist Ideology. The Italian Communists began speaking of the "via italiana al socialismo" (the Italian road to socialism) as distinct from the Soviet model, and Pietro Nenni the PSI leader, issued sharp criticisms of Russian Communism. These years, then, marked an increased absorption of the PCI and the PSI into mainstream political life.

1958 marks the beginning of Italy's "economic boom" in which Italian industrial production became the seventh largest in the world. Italy was now far from a predominately agricultural country. Exports increased dramatically and investment expanded. The European Common Market, established in 1956, was instrumental in stimulating Italian economic vitality. The unequal sharing of this new prosperity, however, created new social problems. Despite the fact that unemployment was significantly reduced, the gap between Northern and Southern Italy actually widened, and thousands of impoverished Southerners emigrated to the northern industrial cities looking for work. The overcrowding, disorientation and crime that this influx caused in the largest northern cities of Milan and Turin became major social and political issues and a recurrent theme in literature and film.

VIII. FILM
IN THE FIFTIES

1. THE HERITAGE OF NEO-REALISM

The neo-realist movement in Italian film was remarkable in the number of directors it enlisted, the unity of political and cultural vision that it possessed and the influence it exerted over film makers throughout the world. Italian neo-realism was part of a broader movement of cultural reconstruction which developed in Europe after the second World War. The rebuilding of European culture was at first inextricably tied to the Resistance experience, the most positive lesson to be drawn from the half-decade of destruction. In France, Germany and Italy the themes of tyranny and rebellion were pervasive in a literature which saw the possibility of a redefinition of cultural values through resistance to oppression. In our discussion of Italian neo-realist literature we have already mentioned the names of Ignazio Silone, Carlo Levi, Elio Vittorini, Cesare Pavese and Vasco Pratolini. All of these novelists shared the commitment to the portrayal of grim, exploitative situations from which rebellious protagonists gain a renewed sense of humanism and meaningful action. Similar themes are evident in German and Italian concentration camp literature such as Ernst Wiechert's *The Forest of the Dead* (1946) Eugen Kogon's *The Theory and Practice of Hell* (1946) and Primo Levi's *Survival at Auschwitz* (1947). In an allegorical vein Albert Camus' famous novel *The Plague* (1947), by tracing a man's fight against disease and death, is also an attempt to define values through opposition and resistance. Most of the above named writers had been actively involved in the underground resistance in World War II and their experiences lent an impressive immediacy to their writings.

Italian neo-realist film, like its counterparts in Resistance literature, insisted that works of art be politically "committed" or "engaged" and served to define values through opposition to tyranny. This was the strength of Resistance culture. It was also its undoing, for when Europe returned to a more normal political and social pattern, the Resistance engagement lost its dramatic appeal. It is no surprise then, that in the early 1950s resistance culture was fading in all of Europe and in all genres. In Italian film the decline of neo-realism was particularly precipitous because a lack of appeal was coupled with government attempts to suppress the movement financially.

The decline of neo-realism is usually equated with a temporary decline in the quality of Italian film in the 1950s. By "decline" one usually means increased imitation, commercialism, predilection for cheap melodrama and an avoidance of serious themes. It is true that Italy relenquished its position as the innovative world leader in film style. No "movement" or "school" with a unified thematic and stylistic vision succeeded the neo-realists in Italy, whereas such movements did arise in France (the *Nouvelle Vague*), England (the Free Cinema), the United States (the Underground), and Brazil (the *Cinema Nôvo*).

This picture of decline must be qualified, however. First of all, many of the "entertainment" or "commercial" films (and the distinction between these and "serious" films is of course problematic in itself) were quite well made, occasionally by some of the masters of the neo-realist period like Vittorio De Sica, Alberto Lattuada and Pietro Germi. Secondly, there was hardly a complete void of films with serious themes, and in fact some of the more notable films of the post-war period were made at this time.

2. THE MAJOR DIRECTORS OF THE FIFTIES

There are four directors who dominate the decade 1950–1960. Two of them, Roberto Rossellini and Luchino Visconti, were former neo-realists who shifted their themes and stylistic technique in the 1950s. The other two were newcomers who became giants in Italian film and achieved international recognition; Michelangelo Antonioni and Federico Fellini.

A. LUCHINO VISCONTI

In 1951 Visconti[11] made *Bellissima (Most Beautiful)* a "soggetto" by Cesare Zavattini, a film which signalled the transition from the political themes of neo-realism to the more psychological themes of the 1950s. *Bellissima* is about a poor Roman mother who dreams of escaping poverty by making a movie star of her little girl. The attempt fails (with rather serious consequences for the child and the mother). The film is like its neo-realist predecessors in its depiction of the family's poverty. Not only are they oppressed economically, they are also victims of the cruel, glamorous myth of sudden success through cinema which tantalizingly offers an escape from gruesome reality. *Bellissima* departs from neo-realism in its greater concentration on the psy-

Cinema Nuovo

Luchino Visconti's *Senso* (1954).

40

chological resonances of the social situation. Most neo-realist films were not concerned with subtle psychological portrayals for they preferred to show the external socio-political aspect of the struggle between rich and poor, Nazis and anti-Nazis, impersonal institutions and individuals. By patiently studying the gradual disillusionment of the mother and the confusion of the child, Visconti looks ahead to subsequent directors whose interests will be predominantly psychological.

In *Senso (Sense)* (1954) based on a 19th century short story by Camillo Boito, Visconti looks at Venice during the Risorgimento, when the Venetians are fighting to drive the Austrians out of their territory and join the newly formed Italian Kingdom. The story revolves around the complication caused by the love affair between an Austrian officer and a Venetian countess whose cousin is involved in the rebellion against Austria. As mentioned in the section on neo-realism, Visconti was from an old aristocratic Milanese family but considered himself a Marxist. This apparent tension in his own background is apparent in *Senso* and subsequent Visconti films. While the Marxist Visconti engages in a rational and progressive analysis of the decline of the aristocracy, the aristocratic Visconti expresses nostalgia for dying aristocratic cultural values. The tension between old and new, nature and reason, detached artist and committed political activist can be seen in *Senso*. Visconti's obsession with decline and aestheticism has occasionally earned him the label of "decadent", but at its best Visconti's decadentism becomes social criticism, as sometimes was true of the Decadent movement in literature at the turn of the century. Social criticism as expression of Visconti's preoccupation with the problem of the South's relation with the North, finds its way also in *Rocco e i suoi fratelli (Rocco and his Brothers)* (1960). Here Visconti faces the challenge of portraying Southern Italian characters, with their passions and values, as he had done earlier in *La Terra Trema*. Here, however, the characters, instead of being shown in their native region, are seen in their difficult search for adjustment in the new environment of the Northern industrial city of Milan. The social problems involved in such a search are, however, sidetracked by Visconti's preference for psychological motivations and melodramatic effect, as can be seen also in his later films, such as Il Gattopardo *(The Leopard)* (1963), *La Caduta degli Dei (The Damned)* (1969), *Morte a Venezia (Death in Venice)* (1970), or *L'Innocente (The Innocent)* (1978).

B. ROBERTO ROSSELLINI

The movement toward psychological over political themes is most pronounced in Roberto Rossellini[12] who in the 1940s made three fine films about the war and in the 1950s made four films with Ingrid Bergman about the lack of communication in personal relationships. These films: *Stromboli,* (1951), *Terra di Dio, (Country of God),* (1951), *Europa 51, (Europe '51),* (1952), *Viaggio in Italia, (Voyage to Italy),* (1953), and *La Paura, (Fear),* (1954) anticipate Antonioni in their use of a female protagonist where anxiety over the impersonal quality of modern society is a catalyst for other characters' "awakening". In Rossellini, however, there is a religious undertone of guilt and redemption that is absent in Antonioni. Rossellini's interest in religion and mysticism is expressed in his *Francesco, Giullare di Dio. (Saint Francis of Assisi),* (1950) and the documentary *India,* (1958). Rossellini, like Visconti abandoned neo-realism in the 1950s, but unlike Visconti Rossellini returned to realism at the end of the decade with two films about the war.

The years 1959–60 witnessed a startling revival of Italian films. One aspect of this revival took the form of a renewal of the Resistance film. The old master of war films Roberto Rossellini made *Il Generale della Rovere, (General della Rovere)* (1959) about the rebellion of Italian prisoners against their fascist captors. In 1960 Rossellini made *Era Notte a Roma, (Nighttime in*

Cinema Nuovo

Roberto Rossellini's *Francesco, Giullare di Dio* (1950).

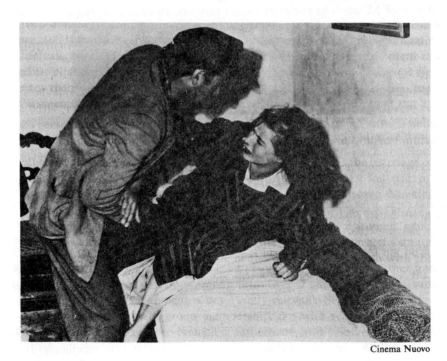

Cinema Nuovo

Roberto Rossellini's *Stromboli* (1951).

Roberto Rossellini's *Europa '51* (1952).

Rome) about a trio of soldiers, a Russian, an American and a British, hiding from the Nazis in occupied Rome.

C. MICHELANGELO ANTONIONI

Although he did not receive worldwide notoriety until the 1960s, Michelangelo Antonioni[13] was well known in Italy after his documentary *Gente del Po, (People of the Po Valley,* (1943). Antonioni was born in Ferrara in 1912 and studied at the University of Bologna. His filmmaking apprenticeship involved a stint at the *Centro Sperimentale di Cinematografia* in Rome in 1942 and work for French director Marcel Carné. He was also a scriptwriter for Rossellini, Visconti, De Santis and Fellini. His first feature film was *Cronaca di un Amore (A Love Story,* 1950), and he also made *I Vinti (The Defeated,* 1952), *La Signora senza Camelie (The Lady Without Camelias,* 1953), *Le Amiche (The Girl Friends,* 1955) and *Il Grido (The Shout, 1957).* In several of these films we find the theme that will unify Antonioni's later work: a concern for the lack of emotional intimacy and meaningful communication in modern society. To depict this void Antonioni employs plots with unresolved mysteries, dialogue which is terse and cold, and long periods of silence.

1959 was the year of Antonioni's major achievement *L'Avventura, (The Adventure)* a story about an architect Sandro, who has forsaken his creative talent in order to get rich through estimates. The story is another one of Antonioni's unsolved mysteries. On a cruise off the coast of Sicily Sandro's girlfriend Anna disappears and is never found. Sandro is aided in his fruitless search for her by Claudia, Anna's friend. Sandro and Claudia become lovers, and as is typical of Antonioni's films the female protagonist, in searching for her own sense of identity draws those

Michelangelo Antonioni's *L'Avventura* (1959).

around her (in this case Sandro) into a period of self-examination. *L'Avventura* is famous for its long sequences which approximate real time as opposed to theatrical time. The slow pace is deliberate, for it makes us live out with the characters their painful experience of loneliness and isolation from one another. *L'Avventura* is, in Antonioni's own words, a dry film, for through the impatience imposed upon the viewer Antonioni tries to communicate the frustration of alienated individuals.

D. FEDERICO FELLINI

Antonioni's films of the 1950s are not well known in the United States. The same is not true for Federico Fellini[14] who earned Academy Awards for Best Foreign Language Film in 1954 with *La Strada (The Road)* and in 1956 with *Le Notti di Cabiria (Cabiria's Nights)*. Fellini lacked Antonioni's formal film training. Born in the Romagna coastal town of Rimini in 1920, Fellini moved to Florence in 1937 where he worked as a cartoonist. A year later he went to Rome where he continued writing cartoon strips and began to write lyrics and routines for the famous vaudeville artist Aldo Fabrizi. During the war Rossellini spotted Fellini drawing silhouettes of American soldiers and employed him as a scriptwriter. In 1950 Fellini co-directed *Luci del Varietà (Variety Lights)* with Alberto Lattuada. In 1952 he made his first solo film, *Lo Sceicco bianco (The White Sheik)* which hilariously debunks the hero of a famous "fotoromanzo" (a type of cartoon strip which uses photographs instead of drawings. *Fotoromanzi* are very popular in Italy and their "stars" are well known). In 1953 Fellini directed the autobiographical *I Vitelloni* (literally "the fat calves") about adolescence in a provincial Italian town. The protagonist Meraldo leaves the town at the end of the film to seek his fortune in the big city, just as Fellini had done. This signals

Federico Fellini's *I Vitelloni* (1953).

a theme which will reappear in several later Fellini films: the contrast between provincial and metropolitan culture and the ambivalence of a protagonist who feels ties to both.

La Strada (*The Road,* 1954) is a haunting drama about a young simpleton girl, Gelsomina, who is bought by a circus-type performer named Zampanò to help with his traveling show. The characters are emblematic: Zampanò is an insensitive brute and Gelsomina is extremely sensitive and innocent. Through a third character, *Il Matto* ("the fool"), another circus performer Gelsomina learns how to break through Zampanò's insensitivity.

In *Le Notti di Cabiria* (*The Nights of Cabiria,* 1956) Fellini's wife Giulietta Masina, who had played Gelsomina in *La Strada* portrays a prostitute who is very naive and innocent. The paradox is intentional: one of Fellini's favorite devices is to depict social "outcasts" such as clowns, prostitutes, simpletons and insane people as wise and prophetic, able to bear a moral message to other characters in the film. This is one of Fellini's ways of attacking the moral pretensions of the rich bourgeois. Both Gelsomina and Cabiria are admonitions to a cynical, over-institutionalized world which ignores simple bonds of love and companionship. For Fellini intensity of emotion is a magic thing, something to be diligently sought amidst an otherwise drab, cold and conventional society. Fellini's films indulge in mysterious, awesome sequences, but not gratuitously, for Fellini feels that magic and love are missing in the world and that they must be restored.

Fellini in 1960 directed the celebrated *La Dolce Vita,* the story of a journalist's gradual decline amidst the high society of Rome. Marcello, the journalist, seems to be Moraldo who left the provincial town in *I Vitelloni* (in fact many of Fellini's films contain cross-references). Fellini and Antonioni are similar thematically in that they are both preoccupied with the lack of modern man's ability to have profound emotional bonds with others. But Fellini's style is greatly different.

He recreates the confusion of his protagonist's life with a rapid whirlwind of humorous, strange and disturbing sequences. And whereas Antonioni's films are devoid of the sacred, Fellini develops a two-pronged religious commentary: he attacks the corruption of modern religious institutions but points out the need for some sense of the transcendant and universal in modern society. In fact, in its "spiritual dryness" modern Rome of *La Dolce Vita* is similar to the London of T. S. Eliot's *The Waste Land*.

3. THE "ABANDONMENT OF NEO-REALISM"

In the 1950s after the decline of neo-realism the majority of Italian films, even the most serious, were not politically oriented. Rossellini, Antonioni and Fellini, in particular, were concerned with problems of a different order. The political "return to normalcy" that characterized Italy in the 50s encouraged this trend. As the politics of centrism dominated the peninsula many reformers, especially intellectuals and artists, lost faith in the ability of politics to change society. Furthermore, many writers and filmmakers asserted that while the problems dealt with by the neo-realists were crucial, there were other important issues that, though undoubtly related to the socio-political environment, were not explicitly political in themselves. The new themes (lack of communication and emotional bonds, excessive industrialization, alienation, etc.) seemed more applicable to the middle class, not the lower classes portrayed in neo-realism. This shift added to the impression that neo-realism had been abandoned. The "abandonment of neo-realism" became a hot issue in the 50s as critics sympathetic to neo-realism (such as Guido Aristarco) attacked Fellini for retreating to a world of dream and fantasy and ignoring the social problems of Italy's oppressed. In the 60s and 70s the political and the psychological will combine to create the novelty of the Italian films of the period.

IX. ITALIAN POLITICAL HISTORY OF THE '60s AND '70s

The most significant event of the 1960s in Italian political history, was the rise of a center-left coalition involving an alliance of the Christian Democrats and the Socialists. It was not an easily reached accord for factions in both parties resisted it and from 1958 to 1962 every attempt to create such a coalition was aborted. But a combination of events in political and religious circles finally wore down the opposition.

Of primary importance was the shift in the attitude of the Vatican which occurred with the election of Angelo Roncalli as Pope John XXIII (1958–1963). One of Pope John's first acts was to remove Luigi Gedda as president of Catholic Action, which weakened the organization's conservative wing. Pope John was deeply concerned with social justice as his famous encyclicals demonstrate: *Mater et magistra* (*Mother and Teacher* 1961) condemned the social and spiritual effects of uncontrolled free enterprise and *Pacem in terris* (*Peace on earth* 1963) endorsed the cooperation of people with different ideological backgrounds in the cause of social justice. The latter was an undisguised reversal of a 1960 article in the Vatican newspaper *L'Osservatore romano,* which had labelled "immoral" any collaboration between Marxists and Catholics. Pope John was seen as harkening back to the 1930s ideals of the French Catholics sympathetic to democratic socialism.

Politically, the DC and PSI showed internal signs of approval of a coalition in 1961 and 1962. The left wing of the DC (with prodding from Aldo Moro), became more influential while the Socialists formally endorsed the NATO alliance. In January of 1961, a center-left coalition (DC-PSI plus smaller parties such as the PRI and PSDI) was established locally in Milan, and Genoa and Florence followed shortly thereafter. In December 1963, the first center-left national cabinet was formed, an arrangement which was to last with varying degrees of tension until 1975.

The year 1968 brought increased complexity to Italian politics, a complexity that reflected new types of unrest in society at large. The most obvious symptom was the student movement and its ties to labor demonstrations. These manifestations of discontent were similar in many ways to their counterparts in France in 1968. But in 1969 a new type of disturbance began to occur: in December 1969, at a bank in Piazza Fontana in Milan, a bomb exploded killing sixteen people and injuring ninety. It was not until 1979 that two neo-Fascists were sentenced for the crime. After several such sporadic emergencies of terrorism, in 1974 the Red Brigade terrorists first came to national attention by kidnapping the Genoese judge Mario Sassi. The Red Brigades, led by Renato Curcio, denounced not only the Christian Democrats but also the Italian Communists, whom they considered too moderate. As the PCI became more and more accepted in daily Italian politics, the ultra-left grew and increasingly denounced what they considered the PCI's abandonment of revolutionary tactics. Red Brigade strategy involved targeting key political commercial and judicial figures for kidnapping, killing or "kneecapping". Their most famous attack came in 1978 against the well-known DC leader Aldo Moro. Moro was kidnapped and executed 55 days later and left in an automobile halfway between the party headquarters of the DC and the PCI, a symbolic and bitter reaction to Moro's efforts to reach an accord between the two parties. Recently the government has had great success in arresting Red Brigade members, particularly after the rescue of the American General Dozier. The members responsible for Aldo Moro's murder have been arrested and brought to trial, and some of them have been sentenced to life imprisonment. On the right wing, extremist violence by such groups as *Ordine Nero (Black Order)* has generally taken the form of random bombings.

Other problems which have plagued Italy in the 1970s were drug-related crimes, the increase of Mafia's interference in social, economic, and political matters, housing shortage, overcrowding in universities, bureaucratic top-heaviness and inefficiency.

As the center-left coalition gradually weakened, there was talk of a new type of alliance, a "historic compromise", between the Christian Democrats and the Communists. This rapprochement was made possible by the PCI's independent position regarding the Soviet Union. The PCI, infact, endorsed NATO and the Common Market, and in February of 1976 Enrico Berlinguer, the head of the PCI, made a remarkable speech in Moscow, declaring the PCI's right to follow a separate, uniquely Italian course within a democratic system. The Italians joined the Spanish Communists in attacking Soviet totalitarianism and asserting the viability of democratic "Euro-communism". In the meantime, the PCI expanded its power base to include large sections of the middle class and Catholics as well. In the central regions of Umbria, Tuscany and Emilia-Romagna, the PCI had been in local government so long that they, not the DC, represented the *status-quo*. The efficiency with which the Communist mayors ran their cities contributed greatly to the party's appeal nationwide. In the 1976 parliamentary elections, the PCI pulled just a few percentage points less than the DC, and by 1978 the PCI had agreed to support many DC proposals in Parliament. But they did not receive any cabinet seats and the leftist faction in the party began to question Berlinguer's patience with the ruling party. They knew that the Socialists had in many ways been hurt by their alliance with the DC and saw similar risks for their own party. PCI-DC collaboration also increased the wrath of the Red Brigades, whose victims were often Communists.

In the late '60s and in the '70s, the political activism of feminist groups succeeded in Italy, as well as in other Western countries, in awakening public opinion to the issues of women's right. Before 1970 Italy had no divorce law. Parliament rectified this situation in 1970 by passing a compromise measure which permitted divorce after a five year waiting period for both consenting parties. In 1974 the Christian Democrats challenged the law by a referendum, but the law was upheld easily. On the issue of abortion, the Parliament passed a liberal abortion law in 1978 which was upheld by the referendum of 1981. Attitudes, of course, cannot be changed by law and legislation, and male dominance has persisted in Italy despite legal measures. Women's rights have become one of the major social issues in Italian politics, literature, and film.

X. FILM IN
THE '60s AND '70s

1. MAIN TRENDS

If the neo-realist period was predominantly political and empirical in its approach and the '50s more psychological and personal, the '60s and '70s combined both tendencies, occasionally in the same film. Indeed, in a culture as politicized as that of modern Italy, it was impossible that the purely subjective themes of the '50s could hold out for long against social criticism. We have noticed that Resistance film revived around 1960 and films about political rebellion in other countries (e.g. *The Battle of Algiers*) and poverty in the South (e.g. *Salvatore Giuliano*) were also made around the same time.

The political films of the '60s, however, were not simply throwbacks to the semi-documentary style of the neo-realist period. In the '60s many directors tried to show the ambiguities and dilemmas of political choice, as opposed to the more Manichaean struggles of the neo-realist period. For example, Gillo Pontecorvo's *La Battaglia di Algeri* (*The Battle of Algiers*, 1966) deals with the Algerian resistance against French occupation forces in the late 1950s. Mathieu, the French commander responsible for quelling the Algerian revolt, is not a stereotypical colonial tyrant. In fact, he himself had been a Resistance rebel in World War II. In a press conference he poses the painful dilemma to the French people: if they want continued rule in Algeria, they cannot have it without violent repression of indigenous dissenters. Mathieu, while carrying out the grisly task of liquidating Algerian guerilla positions in Algiers, is also seen to respect the courage of his foes. Likewise, the Algerian rebels, with whom the film identifies, know that they are not simply killing colonial exploiters; innocent children and adults sometime have to die in guerrilla bombings.

Another fine political film was Francesco Rosi's *Salvatore Giuliano* (1961), a story about a famous Sicilian bandit and an inquest into the interrelation of crime, political interests, and Mafia power on the island. The film was also important at that particular time for bringing the "Southern question" to widespread attention.

Pontecorvo, Rosi, and other political film-makers of the '60s and '70s inherited neo-realism's commitment to social criticism, but injected an increased complexity not only in the political issues involved but in the psychological disposition of the characters. The latter reflected the heritage of the '50s.

Another impetus to the making of political films was the student movement of 1968. Concurrent with this movement was the so-called "cultura di contestazione", or protest culture, which influenced all art forms and which made more sweeping attacks than ever before on contemporary society. No longer content to pick out a particular class or political sector for criticism, many post-1968 writers and directors aimed their attacks at neo-capitalism and consumerism in general, regardless of whether the working class itself be implicated. At times, such criticism went hand in hand with leftist dissent against the moderation of the Italian Communist Party.

2. THE MAJOR DIRECTORS

Most of the famous directors of the '50s continued their work also in the '60s and '70s, such as Visconti, Fellini and Antonioni. Some directors, instead, came to fame in this particular time, such as Pasolini, Bertolucci and Wertmüller. Some of the most renowned Italian films of the '60s and '70s deal with the decadence of a character, of a family, of a social class, of an era. Visconti's films particularly fall into this category.

A. LUCHINO VISCONTI

Visconti's *Il Gattopardo* (*The Leopard*, 1963), based on the famous novel by Giuseppe Tomasi di Lampedusa, depicts Sicily at the time of the "Risorgimento" or Unification, and the effects that this turning point in history had on the Bourbon Prince who must relinquish his power. The approaching death of the Prince is metaphorically extended to the demise of the aristocracy that he represents. Death images pervade the film as the Prince stoically witnesses the end of an era and the rise of the crass, grasping middle class which is replacing him.

In *La Caduta degli Dei* (*The Damned*, 1969), the rise of Nazism in Germany is the background for the moral perversity of the old Essenbeck family, owners of the great steel works of Germany. The Essenbecks are modelled after the Krupp Corporation which supplied Hitler with a substantial part of his armaments. As the family is drawn into vicious internal antagonisms and incestual relationships, the implication grows that there is an inherent connection between Nazism and sexual perversion, a point that drew much criticism from those who felt that Visconti ignored the specific economic, social, and political causes that contributed to the rise of Nazism.

A decadentist approach is also taken in *Morte a Venezia* (*Death in Venice*, 1970), based on Thomas Mann's short novel. Visconti is fascinated with Aschenbach, the protagonist who is beset by his awareness of his own artistic and physical decline and who seeks renewal through the perfect beauty which he finds embodied in a young Polish boy at the Lido in Venice. While *Death in Venice* deals with the decadence of an individual, the following two films by Visconti deal with the decadence of a family, *Gruppo di famiglia in un interno* (*Conversation Piece*, 1974) and of an era, *L'Innocente* (*The Innocent*, 1976). *Gruppo di famiglia* depicts the life of an Italian family in contemporary society and creates a rather bleak view of modern life, plagued by lack of communication, drug addiction and political terrorism. Visconti's last film, *L'Innocente* is an adaptation of a story by the decadentist writer Gabriele D'Annunzio. Here the director's fascination for visual preciosity concentrates masterfully on the description of a fin-du-siècle aristocratic society bound to self-destruction.

B. FEDERICO FELLINI

Fellini followed *La Dolce Vita* with one of his most autobiographical films, *8½* (1963). The title itself is autobiographical: Fellini had previously made six feature length films and had contributed "half" segments to three others, so this was his eighth-and-a-half film. The protagonist is a film director who can no longer decide what type of film he wishes to make, a crisis which is tied in with his problematic relationships with three different women: his wife, his mistress, and an angelic phantasy figure. The story jumps rapidly from present to past, from reality to dream and fantasy. The thematic relationship between love and creativity is, as we can see by now, central to both Fellini and Antonioni. Fellini, however, adds here other themes, such as the authoritarianism of the Roman Catholic Church and its effects on adolescents, the absurdity of the world of film production, and the confrontation between reality and illusion and life and art. Similar themes are present in *Giulietta degli spiriti* (*Juliet of the Spirits,* 1965) which is practically a mirror image of *8½* but with a female protagonist.

Juliet is a middle-aged married woman who has played all her life the role of the "mogliebambina", or child-wife. She is suddenly brought to face reality when she discovers her husband's affair with another woman. She undergoes a series of traumatic experiences which include spiritual seances, encounters with phony oriental prophets, an over-sexed, stunningly beautiful neighbor, and her own inner ghosts. These latter include an overpowering mother-figure, a beloved, rebellious grand-father, and incarnations of Catholic authoritarianism. Eventually Juliet overcomes her ghosts and chases them away. In the last scene of the film, she opens all the windows and doors of her house and steps outside. These actions metaphorically suggest her newly found courage to be herself, to stop hiding inside her home, and to face the world outside.

Fellini Satyricon (1969) and *I Clowns* (1970) are both about decline. The former deals with the decadence of Imperial Rome, and the latter with the disappearance of clowns as an entertainment phenomenon. This disappearance for Fellini means a loss of our ability to laugh at ourselves.

In 1971 Fellini directed *Roma* an impressionistic and autobiographical view of the Italian capital. *Roma* makes a pretense of being a documentary, but what we actually have is Rome as viewed by a green adolescent (the young Fellini) as he arrives there at the height of Fascist rule, and Rome as seen by a middle-aged director (Fellini today). This is hardly Rome of the Touring Club guidebook! It is Rome in the multi-filtered vision of Fellini's memories, fantasies, and imagination. *Roma* overwhelms our senses as it did those of the adolescent Fellini who first stepped down from a train at the central station in 1938. For Fellini Rome is not just a city, but also a second home, a mother, a depository of ancient mysteries and current decadence, of filth, life, death, and renewal. The ending is apocalyptic and pessimistic in its depiction of a new horde of barbarians returning to sack Rome one more time.

Fellini's *Amarcord* (Romagnolo dialect for "Io mi ricordo", *I Remember,* 1974) is similar to *Roma* in its blend of middle-aged recollection of adolescent perceptions. In *Amarcord*, however, the present is never shown and the whole plot concentrates on one year in the life of a young man in a provincial town. As mentioned earlier, Fellini was fascinated by the contrast between provincial and city life. For the adolescent Fellini firmly entrenched in provincial soil, any representation of the outside world was awe-inspiring and legendary. This is why circus performers and vaudeville acts are so prominent in several of Fellini's films: they are the links to the world beyond the horizon. In *Amarcord* such magic passageways to the unknown include the resort hotel with its wealthy exotic guests; an ocean liner; prostitutes who come from other cities; Fascist officials from Rome, movie stars, and race car drivers. All of these are deliberately presented in non-realistic terms, for Fellini is trying to show how they impressed him as an adolescent and how he now recalls those impressions. *Amarcord* is therefore "twice-filtered": through subjective impression and memory. Despite the profound subjectivity of the tale, the film is at the same time Fellini's most political work besides the later *Orchestra Rehearsal*. In *Amarcord* Fellini attacks one of the most subtle and dangerous weapons of Italian Fascism: the program to enlist the loyalty of young males by associating the State (and Mussolini) with virility. Exploiting pubescent sexual fantasies, Fascist propaganda sought to make adolescent boys associate their own developing manhood with the activities and symbols (often sexual) of Fascist youth organizations. Fellini lampoons this pro-

51

gram while occasionally allowing us a glimpse of its tragic side as well. *Amarcord,* then, is a good example of a film which felicitously combines personal and political themes.

Fellini's subsequent production included *Casanova* (1976), *Prova d'orchestra* (*Orchestra Rehearsal,* 1979), and *La Città delle donne* (*The City of Women,* 1981). *Casanova* is a study of the Venetian adventurer and libertine which was not well received critically. *Prova d'orchestra* is a political allegory in which an orchestra in rehearsal acts out the chaos of contemporary Italy. Fellini considered the film a response to the kidnapping and murder of Aldo Moro in 1978. Fellini's most recent film, *La Città delle donne,* is another journey into the past taken by a middle-aged man. This time, however, feminism and some of its most militant proponents provide a foil for the protagonist.

C. MICHELANGELO ANTONIONI

Among Antonioni's films, *L'Avventura* (*The Adventure,* 1959), the story of an architect and his surrender to materialistic pressures, was the first of what has been called Antonioni's "Trilogy of Solitude". The second is *La Notte* (*The Night,* 1960), which also deals with an artist—this time the novelist Giovanni—who feels a diminishing of his own creativity; a problem which is related to the by now listless quality of his marriage. Milan is the setting of this film and Antonioni expertly employs some of the cold, sterile cement backdrop images of the city as metaphors for the cold, sterile relationships between the film protagonists. The third film of the "Trilogy of Solitude" was *L'Eclissi* (*The Eclipse,* 1961), where the lack of communication between the characters is maximized to the point that only objects remain as the main focus of the camera in the last scenes of the film.

All these films were in black and white. With *Deserto Rosso* (*Red Desert,* 1964), Antonioni starts using color, a technique which becomes very powerful in the presentation of the industrial background of the film. *Deserto Rosso* can be viewed as the tragedy of a modern woman, torn between her desires for freedom and independence and her needs for love and security. Giuliana represents the lost soul in the hell of modern industrialization. Her sterile, cold house reflects the unsatisfactory relationship that she has with her husband and son, whom she pampers and serves without developing, however, any real bond of love or respect. The lack of support, both emotional and psychological, which she experiences in her relationship with her weak, un-authoritative husband, produces her mental weakness and fears. At the end, in order to survive, she is reduced to a passive role, inasmuch as she will spend her life avoiding danger and pain, rather than actively facing the problems that life presents.

The next three films were produced directly in English. *Blow-up* (1966) is set in London and deals with a murder story accidentally discovered by a photographer through the photos he had taken in a park. The disconnected and accidental unwinding of the story events reflects the "theater of the absurd" quality of the actions represented in the film. The final scene, where some clowns convincingly play tennis without either rackets or ball, masterfully states the power of art in creating make-belief, while symbolizing at the same time the absurdity of human actions.

The other two films made in the English language were *Zabriskie Point* (1970) and *The Passenger* (1975). The former attempted to capture the sterility of industrial civilization not only through the presentation of the Southern California desert areas, but also through the freeways, ugly streets, office buildings, and the cement landscape of Los Angeles. The film focuses on the conflict between the rebellious and radical younger generation of Diana and Mark and the consumeristic generation of middle-class America at the height of the Vietnam war. Unfortunately the nonprofessionality of the actors and the superficiality of the script marked the film as a failure.

The Passenger is another Antonioni mystery story. In this instance, however, most of the clues are provided and a resolution reached. The story involves a British reporter named Locke, who decides to change his identity by taking on that of a man who has died suddenly of a heart attack in a small hotel somewhere in the African desert. Locke discovers that Robertson, the man whose identity he has stolen, was involved in clandestine arms' sales to African guerillas fighting a war of national liberation. Such an intense commitment (Robertson believed in the cause) is new to Locke, who soon meets a mysterious woman who encourages him to continue Robertson's itinerary. One of Antonioni's favorite themes, that of the search for identity and meaning, is grafted here to a political theme.

D. PIER PAOLO PASOLINI

The 1960s also saw the rise of several new directors. Pier Paolo Pasolini, born in Bologna in 1922, had already established himself as a poet, novelist and essayist. In 1961 he directed his first film, *Accattone* (which is the Roman dialect word for *Beggar*) about the slums in Rome. *Accattone* is a controversial, non-romanticized tribute to and commiseration of slum dwellers, who see no way out of their particular circle of hell. Pasolini was fascinated with the unemployed, despairing poor in these slums and even lived with them for awhile. Indeed, Pasolini considered

Cinema Nuovo

Pier Paolo Pasolini's *Accattone* (1961).

53

himself a Marxist; but if Visconti was a paradoxical aristocrat-communist, Pasolini was a blend of Marxist and religious idealist. There is an attempt in *Accattone* to sanctify the pure violence and despair of the poor by using Bach's Brandenburg Concerto on the soundtrack during particularly gruesome or depressing sequences. Pasolini's religiosity was most unconventional and few among the Italian clergy would have claimed *Accattone* as a religious film. However, even the Church by and large was satisfied with his *Il Vangelo secondo Matteo* (*The Gospel according to St. Matthew*, 1964), which was dedicated to Pope John XXIII. Pasolini's Christ is an angry social reformer as well as spiritual redeemer, one who identifies with the "Accattoni" of his time.

Pasolini's next film was *Uccellacci e Uccellini* (*Hawks and Sparrows*, 1966), a political fable that satirized doctrinaire Marxism. A key character in the film is a talking Marxist crow who has a reply ready for everything. The film is directly related to an issue that had become very important in the Italian Communist Party since Kruschev's famous speech on Stalin and Stalinism in 1956: the amount of self-criticism to be tolerated within party ranks.

Pasolini looked for cinematic topics also in classical mythology and literature, and produced *Edipo re (Oedipus Rex)* in 1967 and *Medea* in 1969. In *Teorema* (*Theorem*, 1968), instead, Pasolini renounces all mythological crutches and creates a work where the middle-class industrial society of our times is harshly criticized because of its lack of moral values. Religious tradition and sexual taboos are also questioned and often violently denounced.

Later on Pasolini returns to traditional literature for the topics of his "trilogy of life": *Il Decameron* (*The Decameron*, 1971), *I Racconti di Canterbury* (*The Canterbury Tales*, 1972), and *Il Fiore delle Mille e una notte* (*The Arabian Nights*, 1973). In *The Decameron* Pasolini modifies the point of view of Boccaccio's work, which was aristocratic and Florentine, by projecting the tales from a Southern Italian popular standpoint and by replacing the elegant Tuscan language of his model with the Neapolitan dialect. What Pasolini maintains and masterfully develops is his model's joy of life and trust in youth, sex, and the natural law. Pasolini himself plays the role of Giotto's best pupil in the film. *The Decameron's* sensational box-office success was repeated by the *Canterbury Tales,* where Pasolini himself portrays Chaucer, and by the *Arabian Nights.*

Pasolini's last work before his tragic death was *Salò o le 120 giornate di Sodoma* (1975), taken from the Marquis de Sade's *120 Days of Sodom*. This work is a reversal of his "triology of life" and deals in a dantesque vision with sadistic power and destructive forces.

E. BERNARDO BERTOLUCCI

Bernardo Bertolucci also began his career in the 1960s. He was an assistant to Pier Paolo Pasolini in *Accattone* and Pasolini's influence is still visible in his first film *La Commare secca* (*The Grim Reaper,* 1962), which is an attempt at handling a detective story in terms of social criticism. His second film *Prima della rivoluzione* (*Before the Revolution,* 1964), like some of Bertolucci's later films, is apparently a political story which develops through existential and psychological motives. The film is partly autobiographical and partly inspired to the French writer Stendhal's *La Chartreuse de Parme.* It deals with the crisis of a disillusioned generation and with the condemnation of the bourgeois society. In the film Bertolucci conducts an examination of the personal, non-political motivations for political action, a theme which had become a favorite of the Italian directors of the '60s and '70s.

Bertolucci sought this union of personal and political themes also in *Il Conformista* (*The Conformist,* 1970). This film adapts to the language of the cinema Alberto Moravia's story of Marcello Clerici who, because of a traumatic homosexual experience in his childhood, devotes his whole life to proving to himself and to others that he is "normal". The ultimate act of defensive conformity is to become an obedient Fascist official and carry out orders to assassinate his former philosophy professor who has become an anti-Fascist leader in Paris. Bertolucci, like other directors of the period, subordinates his interest in politics per se to an exploration of the psychological motivations for political action, motivations which often have nothing at all to do with ideology. Marcello is a conformist, not a Fascist by conviction, as his denunciation of Mussolini after the latter's fall from power demonstrates.

In 1972 Bertolucci reached international renown with his *Ultimo tango a Parigi (Last Tango in Paris)*, where Marlon Brando plays Paul, the male protagonist and Maria Schneider Jeanne, the leading female character. The relationship between Paul and Jeanne begins with a violent sexual copulation in an empty apartment where they meet accidentally while searching for a place to rent. The film ends equally violently when Paul, in his new attempt to transform their brutal, unattached liaison into a romantic one, is killed by Jeanne with her dead father's gun. *Last Tango* probes into the modern myth of total sexuality and discloses its inhuman condition. Communication based on a purely sexual level is doomed to fail inasmuch as the human side of mankind will always search for some forms of relationship also on the sentimental and psychological level.

In *1900* (1976), Bertolucci deals openly again with Fascism as a psychological obsession and perversion, as he had done in *The Conformist*. The epic-length film is set against the background of Socialist peasant risings after World War I and their defeat by the rise of Fascism. The second half of the film carries it up to 1945. In 1900 two male infants, Olmo Dalco, a peasant, and Alfredo Berlinghieri, grandson of the landowner, are born on the same day on the same farm. They grow up as close friends but their different social classes assure tension through their lives, especially after Alfredo becomes *padrone* (Master). The villains are Attila and Regina, the brutal caretakers of the estate who appear as distillations of the Fascist evil mentality. This characterization, like that of the Essenbeck family in Visconti's *The Damned,* invited the criticism that the negative element in Fascism was dealt with as a psychological evil rather than as an ideological and social perversion. This film continues the criticism of the ruling class begun in Bertolucci's earlier film *Before the Revolution* and expands it with an unsympathetic view of the intellectual and his lack of pragmatism in social action.

All throughout Bertolucci's films a tension is sensed towards the father's figure. This disappears in his film *Luna (Moon,* 1979), where it is replaced by an incestuous situation between the female protagonist and her son, a drug addict who does not seem to have any other interest in life outside drugs. Bertolucci returns to his basic interest, the relationship between fathers and sons, in his latest work *La Tragedia di un uomo ridicolo (Tragedy of a Ridiculous Man,* 1981), where the social and political instability of contemporary Italy is also effectively projected through the plot's use of kidnapping, terrorism, and drugs' abuse.

F. LINA WERTMÜLLER

Italian film in the 1970s also boasted the best known of all women film-makers, Lina Wertmüller. She was born in Rome in 1932 of Swiss-Italian descent. Her full name is Arcangela Felice Assunta Wertmüller von Elgg Spanol von Brauchlich!!! Wertmüller worked for Fellini on *8½* and Fellini helped her launch her first film *I Basilischi (The Lizards,* 1963) which dealt with the political situation in Southern Italy and associated the South with Third World Countries in general. The "problema del Mezzogiorno" (Southern Question) is evinced to some degree in all of Wertmüller films, and she tends to relate the political aspects of the Southern Question to the traditional attitude of the Southern Italian male towards women.

Her films include *Mimi metallurgico* (*The Seduction of Mimi*, 1971), *Amore e Anarchia* (*Love and Anarchy*, 1972), *Tutto a posto e niente in ordine* (*All Screwed up*, 1973), *Travolti da un insolito destino nell'azzurro mare d'agosto* (*Swept away*, 1974), *Sette Bellezze* (*Seven Beauties*, 1975) *La fine del mondo nel nostro solito letto in una notte piena di pioggia* (*A Night Full of Rain*, 1977), and *Fatto di sangue fra due uomini a causa di una vedova* (*Blood Feud*, 1978).

The Seduction of Mimi centers upon the character of Mimi, a Southerner who goes to Turin, the industrial capital of Northern Italy, to escape the Sicilian Mafia and find a job as metal worker. Although married in his native Sicilian town, he falls in love with Fiore, a Northern girl, and has a son from her. Once back in his own town, while keeping Fiore and the baby in an apartment, he reenters his family life and resents the fact that his wife has had an affair with another man while he was away and is now pregnant. Unwilling, however, to accept the Sicilian code of *vendetta* (vengeance) which would require him to kill his sexual opponent, he takes upon himself to repay his rival with the same coin by seducing his wife. When the moment of recognition comes, Mimi, however, becomes a scapegoat, as he is accused of killing his rival—shot down by a Mafia hitman—and is sentenced to prison. Several themes connected with contemporary Italian problems, play in this film: the Mafia's oppressive role on the life of any individual who does not want to

Cinema Nuovo

Lina Wertmüller's *Mimi Metallurgico* (1971).

56

conform, the tension between Southern and Northern Italians, the code of *vendetta* which obsesses the Southern male, and the patent inequality for what concerns men's and women's rights.

This last theme becomes predominant in *Love and Anarchy* where it is emphasized by the historical background of the story set in Fascist Italy of the 1930s. As the title suggests, love and politics play an essential role in the story of a young man who comes to Rome as an anarchist in order to kill Mussolini and becomes a guest in one of the most fashionable whore-houses of the capital. The Fascist myth of male virility is amply deployed here together with its corollary, by which the only function of woman on earth is that of a whore. Wertmüller's handling of the two main female characters poignantly underscores the dramatic conflict that arises in intelligent and sensitive women faced with an economic and political situation which does not leave them any other choice of life but in a brothel.

Fascist and Nazist oppression and its destructive influence upon all kinds of human beings are played up again in *Seven Beauties,* where Pasqualino's dis-humanizing experience in concentration camp strips him forever of any redeeming human feature.

In *Swept Away,* the rigid constraints of class and political differentiations that divide the two protagonists of the story at the beginning, the Southern Italian sailor Gennarino and the rich Milanese socialite Raffaella, are shattered by their experience as shipwrecked on an uninhabited island. The myth of primordial man who creates his own paradise with his own two hands and initiative, thus conquering and dominating his female companion, is fully exploited, until civilization takes them both back in again and destroy their primitive union.

Wertmüller's last two films, *A Night Full of Rain* and *Blood Feud,* have been unfavorably received by both public and critics. Her work, however, as a woman director is of paramount importance in Italian film industry where a woman's point of view can effectively reflect the role of Italian women in our contemporary society.

3. OTHER DIRECTORS

Many other films have been made in the '60s and '70s by established directors as well as by film-makers who were previously not too well known especially in the United States. About the established directors, we should mention Vittorio De Sica who, after a long hiatus, returned to political themes with *Il Giardino dei Finzi-Contini* (*The Garden of the Finzi-Contini,* 1970), based on Giorgio Bassani's novel about two Jewish families in Ferrara who feel the increasing threat of Mussolini's 1938 anti-Semitic legislation. In *Una breve vacanza* (*A Brief Vacation,* 1973), De Sica employed many of his neo-realist skills in a story about a female factory worker who is ordered by her doctor to go to a sanatorium in the Alps to cure her lung disease. The title of the film comes from a line by the poet Apollinaire: "Sickness is the vacation of the poor." The film is an excellent synthesis of the themes of poverty and women's exploitation through the character of Clara. It provides also a very fine example of the revival of the neo-realist style in the 1970s.

Concern for the social and political problems of contemporary Italy is expressed in what has been called "political cinema". The main representatives of this trend are Francesco Rosi, Elio Petri, Marco Bellocchio, Vittorio e Paolo Taviani, Ermanno Olmi e Liliana Cavani.

Francesco Rosi's *Cristo si è fermato ad Eboli* (*Christ Stopped at Eboli,* 1979) is an adaptation of the famous story by Carlo Levi about his exile during the Fascist period in a forgotten little town of Southern Italy, plagued by superstition, ignorance, and poverty. The choice of such a theme in a film of the late 1970s hints at the realization that the "Southern Question" has not been resolved yet even after nearly 40 years of democratic government.

Elio Petri digs into different levels of social injustice: police bureaucracy and inefficiency in *Indagine su un cittadino al di sopra di ogni sospetto* (*Investigation of a Citizen above Suspicion*, 1969); the automatism of modern dishumanizing industrial conditions in *La classe operaia va in paradiso* (*The Working Class goes to Heaven*, 1971); or political conformism in *Todo Modo* (*One Way or Another*, 1976), an adaptation of a novel by the Sicilian writer Leonardo Sciascia.

Marco Bellocchio moves from the internal problems of a conservative middle-class family in *Pugni in tasca* (*Fits in the Pocket*, 1965), to political criticism in *La Cina è vicina* (*China is near*, 1967) and eventually to denunciation of religious education in *Nel nome del Padre* (*In the Name of the Father*, 1971).

Padre-Padrone (*Father-Boss*, 1977) is a powerful film by the brothers Taviani, based on the biography of Gavino Ledda, a professor of Linguistics who grew up without any formal education in the Sardinian countryside. While Taviani's film deals with Sardinian shepherds, Ermanno Olmi's *L'Albero degli zoccoli* (*The Tree of the Wooden Clogs*, 1978) describes the hard life of Northern farmers in the Po valley and their social and economic exploitation.

An important woman director is Liliana Cavani whose first two television works, *Francesco d'Assisi* (*Francis of Assisi*, 1966) and *Galileo* (1968) produced very controversial responses because of the unorthodox treatment of the life of their heroes. Cavani's best known film is *Il portiere di notte* (*Night Porter*, 1974), which deals with a greatly disturbing erotic relationship between an ex-Nazist criminal and one of his former victims who survived the concentration camp experience. The problem of good and evil and the individual choice that each human being is requested to make are dealt with also in Cavani's later films *Al di là del bene e del male* (*Beyond Good and Evil*, 1977), an examination of Friedrich Nietzche's life and *La Pelle* (*The Skin*, 1981), an adaptation of Curzio Malaparte's book about Naples during the American occupation.

Two other contemporary directors have been moving into the spotlight of international fame in these last two decades, Franco Brusati and Ettore Scola. Brusati's *Pane e cioccolato* (*Bread and Chocolate*, 1973) is a powerful exposé of the Italian immigrants in Switzerland, their frustrations and defeats, together with their courage and sensitivity which allow them to overcome even the bleakest of all circumstances. Ettore Scola's *Una giornata particolare* (*A Special Day*, 1977), combines the denunciation of Fascist propaganda and political oppression together with the theme of women's exploitation.[15]

NOTES
AND REFERENCES

1. Erich Auerbach, *Mimesis,* Princeton, Princeton University Press, 1968, p. 463.
2. André Bazin, *What is Cinema?,* Berkeley, University of California Press, 1971, p. 19.
3. H. Stuart Hughes, *The United States and Italy,* New York, Norton, 1968, p. 83.
4. Quoted in Pierre Leprohon, *The Italian Cinema,* New York, Praeger, 1971, p. 98.
5. Quoted in P. Hovald, *Le Néo-réalisme italien et ses créateurs,* Paris, Cerf, 1959, p. 201. (Translated by Craig Kelly).
6. Quoted in A. Canziani, and C. Bragaglia, *La stagione neorealista,* Bologna, Cooperativa Libraria Universitaria Editrice, 1976, (Translated by Craig Kelly).
7. Quoted in Roy Armes, *Patterns of Realism,* Cranbury, New Jersey, A. S. Barnes and Co., Inc., 1971, p. 169.
8. *Films and Filming,* March 1961, pp. 31–32.
9. H. Stuart Hughes, *The United States and Italy,* p. 81.
10. Denis Mack Smith, *Italy, A Modern History,* Ann Arbor, The University of Michigan Press, 1969.
11. Pio Baldelli, *I Film di Luchino Visconti,* Lacaitra, Mondina, 1965.
12. Pio Baldelli, *Cinema dell'ambiguita': Rossellini, De Sica, Zavattini, Fellini,* Rome, Samone e Savelli, 1971.
13. Pierre Leprohon, *Michelangelo Antonioni, An Introduction,* Simon and Schuster, New York, 1963.
14. Edward Murray, *Fellini the Artist,* New York, Federick Ungar Publishing Co., 1976.
15. For an exhaustive study of Italian film, see the excellent book by Peter Bondanella, *Italian Cinema: From Neorealism to the Present,* Ungar Publ. Co., New York 1983.

TIME LINE

1922

    Politics: —Mussolini comes to power

1925

    Film: —L.U.C.E. established

1932

    Film: —*Men, What Scoundrels!*   (Camerini)

1933

    Politics: —Hitler comes to power in Germany
    Literature: —*Fontamara*   (Silone)

1935

    Politics: —Italy invades Ethiopia
    Film: —C.S.C. founded
                   —*Cinema* founded
                   —*I'll Give a Million*   (Camerini)

1936

    Politics: —Annexation of Ethiopia
                   —Rome-Berlin Axis

1937

    Politics: —Death of Antonio Gramsci
    Literature: —*Bread and Wine*   (Silone)
    Film: —*Bianco e nero* founded

1938

    Politics: —Chamber of Fasces and Corporations
    Literature: —Pratolini's first short stories

1939

    Politics: —Italy occupies Albania
                   —"Pact of Steel" joins Italy and Germany in
                      military alliance
                   —Germany invades Poland; beginning of World
                      War II
    Film: —*A History of Cinema from its Origins to the Present* (Pasinetti)

1940

    Film: —*The Iron Crown*   (Blasetti)
                   —Cineteca Italiana founded in Milan
                   —Milan Triennale

1941

    Literature: —*In Sicily*   (Vittorini)
    Film: —*Little Old Fashioned World*   (Soldati)
                   —*The Hospital Ship*   (Rossellini)

1942		
	Literature:	—Vittorini publishes *Anthology of American Literature*
	Film:	—Several important articles on realism in *Cinema*
		—*The Children are Watching Us* (De Sica)
		—*Four Steps Among the Clouds* (Blasetti)
		—*Ossessione* (Visconti)
		—Pasinetti's Venice documentaries
1943		
	Politics:	—Allied invasion of Sicily
		—Mussolini falls; Badoglio takes over
		—CLN organized in Rome
		—Italy signs Armistice with Allies
1944		
	Politics:	—The "Battle for Rome" May 11-June 1
	Film:	—*Cinema* branch of CLN founded in Rome
1945		
	Politics:	—Mussolini captured on April 27 and executed the following day
1945		
	Politics:	—First post-war government of Francesco Parri gives way in December to coalition government headed by Alcide De Gasperi
	Literature:	—*The Naked Streets* (Pratolini)
	Film:	—*Rome Open City* (Rossellini)
1946		
	Politics:	—Italy proclaimed a Republic
	Literature:	—*A Tale of Poor Lovers* (Pratolini)
	Film:	—*Paisà* (Rossellini)
		—*To Live in Peace* (Zampa)
		—*The Bandit* (Lattuada)
		—*Shoeshine* (De Sica)
		—Cannes Film Festival shows several neo-realist films
1947		
	Politics:	—De Gasperi forms a Cabinet without the Socialists and Communists
		—The Marshall Plan
	Film:	—*Germany in the Year Zero* (Rossellini)
		—*Pursuit* (De Santis)
		—*In the Sunshine of Rome* (Castellani)

1948

    Politics: —April Elections reaffirm Italian government's
                     shift to the right

Film:	—*La Terra trema*	(Visconti)
	—*Bicycle Thieves*	(De Sica)
	—*Bitter Rice*	(De Santis)
	—*In the Name of the Law*	(Germi)
	—*Without Pity*	(Lattuada)

1949

    Politics: —Italy's economy shows significant signs of recovery
                   —Andreotti Law

Film:	—*No Peace Among the Olives*	(De Santis)
	—*Springtime*	(Castellani)
	—*The Mill on the Po*	(Lattuada)

1950

Film:	—*The Road of Hope*	(Germi)
	—*Variety Lights*	(Lattuada-Fellini)
	Francesco Giullare di Dio	(Rossellini)
	Cronaca di un amore	(Antonioni)

1951

Film:	—*Achtung Banditi!*	(Lizzani)
	Bellissima	(Visconti)
	Stromboli	(Rossellini)
	Terra di Dio	(Rossellini)
	—*Cinema* becomes *Cinema nuovo* under the	
	direction of Guido Aristarco	

1952

Film:	—*Umberto D.*	(De Sica)
	—*Two Pennyworth of Hope*	(Castellani)
	Europa '51	(Rossellini)
	I Vinti	(Antonioni)
	Lo Sceicco bianco	(Fellini)

1953

    Politics   Passing of the "legge truffa"

Film	*Viaggio in Italia*	(Rossellini)
	La Signora senza Camelie	(Antonioni)
	I Vitelloni	(Fellini)

1954

Film	*Senso*	(Visconti)
	La Paura	(Rossellini)
	La Strada	(Fellini)

1955

    Politics   The *Vanoni* plan

Film	*Le Amiche*	(Antonioni)

1956

Film	*Le Notti di Cabiria*	(Fellini)

1957			
	Film	*Il Grido*	(Antonioni)
1958			
	Politics	Beginning of Italy's "economic boom."	
	Film	*India*	(Rossellini)
1959			
	Film	*Il Generale Della Rovere*	(Rossellini)
		L'Avventura	(Antonioni)
1960			
	Film	*Rocco e i suoi fratelli*	(Visconti)
		Era notte a Roma	(Rossellini)
		La dolce vita	(Fellini)
1960			
	Film	*La Notte*	(Antonioni)
1961			
	Politics	First center-left coalition	
		Pope John's encyclical *Mater et Magistra*	
	Film	*Salvatore Giuliano*	(Rosi)
		L'Eclisse	(Antonioni)
		Accattone	(Pasolini)
1962			
	Film	*La Commare secca*	(Bertolucci)
1963			
	Politics	First center-left national cabinet formed.	
		Pope John's encyclical *Pacem in terris*	
	Film	*Il Gattopardo*	(Visconti)
		8½	(Fellini)
		I Basilischi	(Wertmüller)
1964			
	Film	*Deserto rosso*	(Antonioni)
		Il Vangelo secondo Matteo	(Pasolini)
		Prima della rivoluzione	(Bertolucci)
1965			
	Film	*Giulietta degli Spiriti*	(Fellini)
		Pugni in tasca	(Bellocchio)
1966			
	Film	*La Battaglia di Algeri*	(Pontecorvo)
		Blow up	(Antonioni)
		Uccellacci e uccellini	(Pasolini)
1967			
	Film	*Edipo Re*	(Pasolini)
		La Cina è vicina	(Bellocchio)
1968			
	Politics	Students' movement	
	Film	*Teorema*	(Pasolini)

1969
    Politics   Terrorists' attack on Piazza Fontana.

1969		
Politics	Terrorists' attack on Piazza Fontana.	
Film	*La Caduta degli Dei*	(Visconti)
	Fellini Satyricon	(Fellini)
	Medea	(Pasolini)
	Indagine su un cittadino al di sopra di ogni sospetto	(Petri)
1970		
Politics	Divorce Law passed by Parliament	
Film	*Morte a Venezia*	(Visconti)
	I Clowns	(Fellini)
	Zabriskie Point	(Antonioni)
	Il Conformista	(Bertolucci)
	Il Giardino dei Finzi-Contini	(De Sica)
1971		
Film	*Roma*	(Fellini)
	Il Decameron	(Pasolini)
	Mimi metallurgico	(Wertmüller)
	La Classe operaia va in paradiso	(Petri)
	Nel Nome del Padre	(Bellocchio)
1972		
Film	*The Canterbury Tales*	(Pasolini)
	L'Ultimo Tango a Parigi	(Bertolucci)
	Amore e Anarchia	(Wertmüller)
1973		
Film	*The Arabian Nights*	(Pasolini)
	Tutto a posto e niente in ordine	(Wertmüller)
	Una breve vacanza	(De Sica)
	Pane e cioccolato	(Brusati)
1974		
Politics	Referendum on Divorce	
	First Red Brigades' kidnapping	
Film	*Swept away*	(Wertmüller)
	Il portiere di notte	(Cavani)
	Gruppo di famiglia in un interno	(Visconti)
	Amarcord	(Fellini)
1975		
Film	*The Passenger*	(Antonioni)
	Salò	(Pasolini)
	Sette Bellezze	(Wertmüller)
1976		
Politics	Enrico Berlinguer's speech in Moscow on PCI's right to follow its own cause.	
Film	*L'Innocente*	(Visconti)
	Casanova	(Fellini)
	1900	(Bertolucci)
	Todo Modo	(Petri)

1977			
	Film	*A Night full of Rain*	(Wertmüller)
		Padre-Padrone	(Taviani)
		Al di là del bene e del male	(Cavani)
		Una giornata particolare	(Scola)
1978			
	Film	*Blood Feud*	(Wertmüller)
		L'Albero degli zoccoli	(Olmi)
1979			
	Film	*Prova d'orchestra*	(Fellini)
		Luna	(Bertolucci)
		Cristo si è fermato ad Eboli	(Rosi)
1981			
	Politics	Referendum on abortion	
	Film	*La città delle donne*	(Fellini)
		La tragedia di un uomo ridicolo	(Bertolucci)
		La pelle	(Cavani)

MAP OF ITALY